# UP WITH SKOOL!

*Children's own choice of
the best school jokes*

**Pictures by Quentin Blake**

**PUFFIN BOOKS**

Puffin Books, Penguin Books Ltd, Harmondsworth, Middlesex, England
Penguin Books, 625 Madison Avenue, New York, New York 10022, U.S.A.
Penguin Books Australia Ltd, Ringwood, Victoria, Australia
Penguin Books Canada Ltd, 2801 John Street, Markham, Ontario, Canada L3R 1B4
Penguin Books (N.Z.) Ltd, 182–190 Wairau Road, Auckland 10, New Zealand

First published 1981
Published simultaneously in hardback by Kestrel Books

Made and printed in Great Britain by
Richard Clay (The Chaucer Press) Ltd, Bungay, Suffolk
Set in Monophoto Ehrhardt by
Northumberland Press Ltd, Gateshead, Tyne and Wear

# Contents

# *Introduction*

FATHER: Well, Tracy, what did you learn on your first day at school?

TRACY: Not enough, Dad, I've got to go back tomorrow!

Schooldays may or may not be the happiest of your life – but judging by the jokes in this book, they are certainly among the funniest. When we invited classes from all round the country to send in their favourite jokes on ten special school themes, we expected plenty about teachers and games and school dinners. But punishment? And homework? In fact we got hundreds on both subjects. It seems that children can raise a laugh even on subjects which they find ... well, painful.

Perhaps we shouldn't have been surprised by the response. School is the one major shared experience of all children, and they get little enough opportunity to express their feelings about it. Playground humour is more than just a joke – it's an indication of what children really think about school. And that humour has come to this book directly from the playgrounds themselves. I'd like to thank the schools who participated (about 200 altogether), especially those dozen or so who used the collecting of material as a classroom project. A complete listing of participating schools is given on pages 156–60.

How did we contact the schools in the first place? Appeals for jokes were made by the *Sunday Times* START HERE pages, *Child Education* and *The Times Educational Supplement*; by the magazines of the Puffin Club and the

Australian Puffin Club (*Puffin Post* and *Puffinalia*); by the Puffin Federation of Bookclubs; by many local news-papers, including the *Birmingham Evening Mail*, *Halifax Advertiser*, *South London News* series, *Surrey Press* and *Wrexham Evening Leader*; and also by Books for Students, the book wholesaler which supplies many school book-shops. In addition, the following local radio stations featured the search for jokes: Birmingham, Blackburn, Brighton, BRMB, Foyle, Manchester, Medway, Newcastle, Nottingham, Scotland and Trent. Without these organi-zations the book would not have been possible.

I would also like to acknowledge the work of the Puffin team who had the immense task of collating and selecting the jokes: Patricia Burgess, Anne Rowell and especially Philippa Dickinson, who not only appeared on numerous radio stations around the country, but also had the final, seemingly impossible, task of reducing the enormous amount of material to a manageable and coherent manu-script.

Finally, thanks to our ten celebrities who wrote pieces about their own schooldays. Their work stands for itself: in its mixture of affection, distaste and humour, it perfectly complements the jokes from the children themselves.

TONY LACEY
Puffin Chief Editor

# Gruesome
# Games

## *Gruesome Games* by Harry Secombe

*Harry Secombe began his goonish career at St Thomas's Junior School, Swansea, and Dynevor School, Swansea.*

If anyone ever asks me what my favourite subject was in school I always say 'Games'. That was the time I liked best – when we were let out of the chalk-riddled atmosphere of the classroom into the fresh air of the playground. There was only one drawback – the surface of the yard was covered with asphalt, and every time we fell down it really hurt. To this day, if my memory fails me about my schooldays, I just run my fingers over my knees or my elbows and the memories come flooding back as I feel there the scars I acquired playing soccer, rounders, cricket, leapfrog or rugby. Especially rugby, because I was brought up in Swansea, South Wales, and any boy who did not play our national game was a 'cissy'.

I have to confess, though, that I was not very good at games. From the age of seven I had to wear spectacles to correct my short-sightedness and I was always afraid of getting them broken. It was pretty impossible to play without them, so I always held back from tackling and would give up the ball very quickly when challenged. There was one day, though, when I actually scored a goal. This was when I had progressed to Dynevor Secondary School, which boasted a grass playing field and real goal-posts, not coats placed apart on the ground.

We were playing another class at soccer and I was right back. That was as far away from the action as I could get without actually being behind the goal-mouth. As we were the third team, we had to take whatever jerseys were left over and both sides wore a variety of colours.

I was dawdling near the touchline talking to a friend who had come to see me play because he needed a laugh – his hamster had just died – when a horde of yelling lunatics descended on me and I found myself lying face down in the mud with my spectacles broken and both nostrils plugged with Welsh turf. The referee, our sports master, sent me back to the pavilion to try to sort myself out. My friend, who was now hysterical with laughter, came with me, his dead hamster forgotten. It was useless trying to repair my shattered glasses and once I had cleared out my nose I decided to go back onto the field again, if only to get rid of my cackling companion.

I peered uncertainly about me as I took up the position I had left. All the other players were up the far end again, and I jumped up and down on the spot to keep warm. Suddenly, without warning, I found the ball at my feet. It had somehow been kicked all the way from the distant end of the pitch. Not knowing quite what to do I began to dribble it in a somewhat desultory fashion towards the other goal. To my surprise I met with little resistance and with a pounding heart slammed the ball into the net. A goal!

I turned and squinted towards my fellow players, expecting hands thudding congratulations on my back. Instead my captain rushed up to me shouting 'You fool, Secombe, you fool!'

'What d'you mean?' I said puzzled at the non-reaction. 'I've scored a goal.'

'It's an *own* goal,' screamed my captain. 'We

changed sides for the second half when you were in the dressing room.'

That was the last time I ever played soccer. I wasn't really sorry though – I was into cricket by the time spring came around. You see, they needed a sight-screen.

TEACHER: Alec, why does having a dream about a football match make you late for school?
ALEC: Because they played extra time, Sir.

P.E. TEACHER: Why didn't you stop that ball?
GOALIE: That's what the net's for isn't it?

TEACHER: Why are you only wearing one glove in goal?
BOY: Well, Sir, the weather forecast said it might be cold, but on the other hand, it might be hot.

'Sir, I don't like the colour of the football.'
'Kill it.'
'What, dye it a different colour?'

'What position do you think I play in football?'
'Left back?'
'Left back in the changing rooms.'

FOOTBALLER: I have a good idea on how to improve our team.
GAMES TEACHER: Good, are you leaving?

Knock, knock.
Who's there?
Penny.
Penny who?
Penalty pass against goal shooter.

TEACHER (*on returning from football practice*): Has any-
one seen my glasses?
PUPIL: Yes, Sir, you left them on the pitch.
TEACHER: Silly boy, why didn't you give them to me?
PUPIL: I didn't think you'd want them after I'd stepped
on them!

TEACHER: Sporty, give me a sentence using the word
'indisposition'.
SPORTY: I always play goalie because I like playing indisposition.

TEACHER: How many seasons in a year?
BOY: Two, Sir. Football and cricket!

'What team do you support?'
'I support my legs because they support me.'

Two school football teams were going to play in the final
of the local cup competition. One headmaster said that
for every goal his team scored he would excuse them from

14

one evening's homework. The other headmaster said that he would give five minutes extra playtime for every goal his school scored. The captains shook hands, had a quick chat, and tossed the coin. At half time the score stood at 72–70.

There were two boys playing football. One boy tried for a goal and missed and said, 'I could kick myself.'
His friend said, 'Don't bother, you'll probably miss.'

PUPIL: Sir, I want to have a lot of practice of football today.
TEACHER: Well, you're very lazy, so have a practice at headball, it might affect your brains more than my lessons do!

'Our school team has got two new Chinese footballers.'
'Chinese footballers?'
'Yes, We Won Once and How Long Since.'

DAD: I hear you are in the school football team, son. What position are you?
SON: The games master says I am the main draw back.

FATHER: You used to like football at school; why don't you enjoy it any more?
JIMMY: Every time we score a goal, the teacher stops the game to rehearse the action replays.

JILL: I 'ate games.
JOHN: Really – what do they taste like?

What is the best way to play your favourite game in school?
*Break the rules.*

In a football match the referee was heard to say: 'Free kick – and I don't mean the opposition.'

New football programme for schools:
*When the Boot Comes In.*

BOY: If there's a referee in football, and an umpire in cricket, what is in bowls?
TEACHER: I don't know.
BOY: Goldfish.

TEACHER: We are all going to play squash. Billy, which side would you like to play on?
BILLY: The Oranges' side, please.

There once was a great huge cat,
Who swallowed a whole cricket bat.
He swallowed the ball,
The wickets and all –
The cricket team clobbered him flat.

Why was the cricket team given lighters?
  *Because they kept losing their matches.*

When is cricket a crime?
  *When there's a hit and run.*

What can you serve, but not eat?
  *A tennis ball.*

BOY: When was tennis mentioned in the Bible?
TEACHER: I don't know.
BOY: When Joseph served in Pharaoh's court!

Why are tennis balls round?
  *Because if they were square they would not roll.*

There was a contest at our school once to see who was the best boxer. In the first round, a bad boxer was swinging punches like fury but not landing any. At the end of the round he asked the games master if he was getting anywhere.

'No,' replied the games master, 'but keep on with what you're doing – he might feel the draughts and catch a cold!'

What ring is square?
  *A boxing ring.*

I know it's dangerous to swim on a full stomach, so after lunch I always swim on my back.

What do you get when you cross a dive with a handstand?
*A broken back.*

Which game goes round and round?
*Rounders.*

Why did Cinderella get thrown out of the rounders team?
*Because she kept running away from the ball!*

What has eleven heads and runs around screaming?
*A school hockey team.*

Why is the hockey pitch always wet?
*Because the girls are always dribbling.*

What did the games teacher say to the girl who lost a hockey ball?
*Find it quickly, or I'll give you the stick.*

Why does J.R. play hockey?
*Because he likes to bully.*

SPORTS MASTER: Why didn't you attempt the high jump?
BOY: Because I'm scared of heights.

TEACHER: Why didn't you jump the long jump, boy?
BOY: But Sir, I'm short-sighted.

SPORTS TEACHER: Bobby, why did you refuse the long jump?
BOBBY: Well, Sir, I'm allergic to sand.

'I've got a terrible cold. I won't be able to do the high jump.'
  'Why not?'
  'I can't even clear my throat.'

What does the winner lose in his race?
  *His breath, of course!*

A girl rushed into the house from school and said excitedly, 'Mum, I think I might be in the school athletics team.'
  'Why?'
  'Today our teacher said that if I go on as I have been doing, I'll be for the high jump.'

Why did the liquorice go jogging?
  *Because it was a liquorice-all-sport.*

Why is it funny to see a boy run a mile?
  *Because he really moves just two feet.*

What does P.T. stand for?
  *Physical Torture.*

Two brothers were talking about their school. The younger one said, 'I'm fed up with the P.E. teacher.'
  'Why?'
  'He has one answer to all our problems, "Gym'll Fix It."'

BOY: Dad, will you get me a pair of pumps for gym, please?
DAD: He can buy his own, can't he?

Why did the boy who was balancing on the bar give up?
  *Because his performance began to fall off.*

What do you call the man who takes you for P.E.?
> *Jim Nast.*

He drives us up the wall
And puts us through the hoop.
We never have a ball,
To that he wouldn't stoop.
He really makes us crawl,
To him we bend the knee,
But with our arms outstretched
We worship our P.E.

My class was doing some P.E. training. We did ten laps around the school. When a slow boy finally got back he asked the teacher, 'Did you take my time?'
> 'No', said the teacher, 'you did.'

'Get on the apparatus, children,' said the teacher in the gym. There was a ray of hope for Johnnie as he stood there on the sun beam.

Our Chinese golf teacher's an expert.
> *He's called Ho Lin Wun.*

What is the quietest game?
> *Ten pin bowling, because you can hear a pin drop.*

Dear Mr Williams,
> John will not be able to play games because he has a bad chest.
> Yours sincerely,
> *My mother.*

GAMES TEACHER: You never come first in anything.
PUPIL: I always come first in the dinner queue.

Two junior school rugby team players talking:
1ST BOY: You know that rugby team called 'The Wasps'?
2ND BOY: Yeah!
1ST BOY: Do you think they've got a 'B' team?

A little boy said to his friend, 'I know how to service my pogo stick.'
    'How?'
    'Give it a spring clean.'

*Games* by Buck A. Springer
*Bad Striker* by Mr Goal
*Careless Jockey* by Betty Felloff
*P.E.* by Jim Nastic
*Better Gym* by Horace Zontalbars
*Neck Exercise* by G. Raffe

# *Delicious*
# *Dinners*

### *Delicious Dinners* by
### Cyril Smith, M.B.E., M.P.

*Spotland Primary School, Rochdale Open Air School
and Rochdale Municipal High School for Boys saw the
early years of one of Rochdale's most famous sons.*

It will not surprise you when I tell you that food is very
dear to my heart. Dear, that is, in a loving sense rather
than an expensive one. Mind you, when I recently dined
at Oulder Hill School in Rochdale, the Head did assure
me that he was prepared to accept American Express
Cards!

Actually, I found the food very enjoyable. It was
always enjoyable when I was a schoolboy myself – but
my word, what a difference there now is. You actually
have a choice of menu! I was offered beefburgers,
salads, cheese and onion pastie and so on. I could have
chips, peas, baked beans and there were pickles of
various sizes and flavours. For sweet, it was ice-cream,
cheese and biscuits or flan – and whilst water was free,
you could purchase coke or orangeade! The food was,
incidentally, excellent and I thoroughly enjoyed it.

When I was a lad (and that is getting more and more
distant), you had chips once a week. Potato mash was
the four-day diet, with mince meat, or roast beef, potato
pie and crust, hot pot, steamed fish, shepherds pie and
so on. For sweet it was rice pudding, semolina or roly
poly jam and custard. You'd a fair idea what would be
on each day in advance, indeed, each week in advance –
because the menu was a rolling one weekly!

I went, for twelve months, to a school for delicate

23

children (yes – honestly!), and there the food was very much a part of our education, as was the midday enforced rest in bed, and the fresh air in abundance. The food was to build us up physically – and you may think they didn't do a bad job!

Later in life, I became Chairman of the Education Committee. I remember once having to visit a meals centre that was having trouble with the children. I went to 'quell' the 'threatened riot'. A cartoon published later depicted me standing at the door, the children at their meal tables – and it carried the caption 'The Ultimate Deterrent'.

I remember the coffee once served to me in a school by a fourteen-year-old child. She had clearly been taught to ask whether the visitor wanted black or white coffee, and so she asked me, 'Black or white, sir?' 'Black, please,' I replied, and said I would pour my own. I was filling up my cup with black coffee when she said 'Hang on, sir, leave a bit of room for't milk!'

'Cook, cook, there's some feathers in my custard.'
'Yes I know, it's Bird's custard.'

'Cook, cook, there's a dead fly in my soup.'
'Yes, it's the hot water that kills them.'

PUPIL: There's a fly in my soup.
DINNER LADY: So there is. That'll be 20p extra, please.

BOY: What's that fly doing in my gravy?
DINNER LADY: Looks like the breast stroke.

BOY: There are bees in my soup!
DINNER LADY: That's all right – it's alphabet soup.

'Dinner lady, dinner lady, there's a slug on my cabbage.'
'Shhh! Or everybody will want some meat.'

MARK: Oooh! There's a small beetle in my potato!
DINNER LADY: Sorry, I'll fetch you a bigger one.

What did the boy say to the dinner lady?
> *This soup's so lumpy, even the flies are rock climbing.*

Define a school chip.
> *A micro-concrete post.*

'I say, I say, I say, what did the school dinner say to the
   pudding?'
'Nothing; dinners and puddings don't talk.'

There was salad for school dinner, so how did they say
   grace?
> *Lettuce pray.*

What tables don't you have to learn?
> *Dinner tables.*

What's the difference between school dinners and a bucket
   of pig swill?
> *School dinners come on a plate, not in a bucket.*

What do you call a Scotsman who delivers school meals?
> *Dinner Ken.*

Can school peas get married?
> *Not if they're Batchelors'.*

What do you get when you cross rotten eggs with spaghetti?
>*School dinners.*

Why do dinner ladies wear overalls?
>*So when you flick food at them, they don't get it all over their clothes.*

Why do cave men eat school potatoes?
>*Because they are made out of rock.*

What did the front teeth say to the back teeth?
>*Look out, here comes the school dinner.*

How do school puddings start their races?
>*Sago.*

Comment on school dinners: What goes down, must come up!

BILLY: Hey Pete, I wouldn't eat that gravy – it bonds in three seconds!

'I won't say school dinners are bad, but if you gave marks for them, they'd get 1/10 and be made to do it again.'

COOK: And did you enjoy today's toffee tart?
PUPIL: Mmmmmmmmmm!

BILL: I thought you said there was a choice of greens, Miss.
DINNER LADY: There is.
BILL: Well, what's the choice? I can only see one type of vegetable.
DINNER LADY: The choice is take it or leave it.

DINNERLADY: If you eat another of those sausages you'll burst.
CHILD: Too late, I've eaten one already, so stand back.

DINNER LADY: Eat up your cabbage, Jim, it will bring colour into your cheeks.
JIM: But I don't want green cheeks.

COOK: You don't appreciate good food.
BOY: I haven't tasted any yet.

DINNERLADY: Come on, eat up your custard.
PUPIL: I can't, the mice are using it as a trampoline.

TEACHER: Why did you mop up your milk with your cake?
BOY: Because it's a sponge cake.

If you eat school dinners, you'll never live to regret it.

There was a school boy named Freddie,
Who ate several helpings of jelly
Then rhubarb and custard
And sausages with mustard,
Which gave him a pain in his belly!

TEACHER: Sorry, children, school dinners are going up
again.
GIRL: Where to? The ceiling?

DINNER LADY: Do you want seconds?
BOY: No, I'm too young to die.

TEACHER: Eat up your dinner, it's full of iron.
PUPIL: No wonder it's so tough.

Do you know how the school cooks cook baked apples?
*They set the orchard on fire.*

What did Andy Pandy say when he saw his first school
dinner?
*'Time to go home!'*

DINNER LADY: Why are you late for dinner?
PUPIL: Because the bell went too early.

'Miss, my sausage is loud!'
'How come?'
'Because it's a banger.'

Some children like their dinner,
Some other children don't.
But when it comes to cabbage
They turn up their noses and grunt!!!

What did the boy eating school dinner say to the girl?
 *'Hey, that's my finger you're eating.'*

FRED: Why are you hitting that plate with a sausage?
TOM: I want some bangers and SMASH!

Our school cook is so bad, all the cookers have bent legs.

Why couldn't Dracula eat school dinners?
 *He was afraid he might get a steak through his heart.*

A boy was talking to his friend at dinner time. After a while he took some money out of his pocket and ate it. His friend asked why. 'Well,' he said, 'my mum said it was my dinner money.'

Why did the little boy stuff himself with ten dinners?
 *He wanted to be a huge success!*

GIRL: Miss, why have we got square plates?
DINNER LADY: Because we're serving square meals!

1ST BOY: Why do you always have circular sandwiches?
2ND BOY: Because I have a lovely round feeling in my
   stomach.

PUPIL: Can I have some horrible greasy chips, an under-
   done egg, and meat that tastes like an old boot?
DINNER LADY: I couldn't possibly give you anything like
   that!
PUPIL: Why not? That's what you gave me yesterday.

MANDY: Miss, your kitchen must be very clean.
DINNER LADY: How do you know that?
MANDY: Because everything tastes of soap.

BOY: There's no rabbit in this rabbit pie.
DINNER LADY: Well, you would hardly expect a dog in
   a dog biscuit would you?

What is the rudest food we have at school?
   *Sausages, because they spit.*

At dinner-time that day,
I heard the other boys say,
'Look at all the wormies there,
They look like young Billy's hair!'

CHILD: Cook, cook, this egg is bad.
COOK: Well don't blame us, boy, we only laid the table.

BOY: Cook, dinner was awful today! It tasted like glue.
COOK: Well, you should stick to packed lunches.

BOY: What soup is this?
DINNER LADY: It's bean soup, laddie.
BOY: I don't care what it was, I want to know what it is now.

BOY: Give me something to eat please, and make it snappy.
COOK: Will a crocodile sandwich do?

PUPIL: Miss, we had frog's legs for dinner.
TEACHER: Really, what are they like?
PUPIL: Dunno, they hopped away.

Cabbage: seaweed
Ravioli: soggy pillows
Sausages: UFOs
Beans on toast: skinheads on a raft
Cornflakes: dehydrated wheat
Semolina: wallpaper paste
Cauliflower: bits of brains
Spaghetti bolognese: worms in gravy

Beefburgers and mash: shoe soles on cement
Hard-boiled eggs: Kojaks

We played rounders with our rock cakes, but they broke
the bats.

In the school canteen, the dinner lady asked a boy what
he would like.
  'Please, can I have asparagus?'
  'We don't serve sparrows and my name is NOT Gus!'

What did the mayonnaise say when the dinner lady took
  off the lid?
> *'How dare you, I'm dressing!'*

'What did you do with the school custard today?'
'I gave it to the caretaker to use as cement.'

The school dinner was nice today – we used the dumplings
as rounder balls.

I have red hair
Just like spaghetti.
They should have picked on my sister Betty,
Whose hair is also like spaghetti.

What is a better name for school custard?
> *Polycel.*

What's slimy and has eyeballs in it?
> *School tapioca.*

What did Flash Gordon have for his school dinner?
> *Flashed potatoes.*

How does Batman's teacher call him in for his dinner?
> *'Dinner, dinner, dinner, dinner, dinner, dinner, dinner,
> dinner Batman.'*

There was an old man of Poole,
Who had one day at school.
He ate a school dinner,
Which made him much thinner,
That poor old man of Poole.

There was a young boy from Crewe,
A Cheshire lad, hearty and true.
He ate a school dinner
And he was the winner
Of the race to reach the loo.

There was a greedy young fellow named Sid,
Who ate school tarts for a quid.
When they asked, 'Are you faint?'
He replied, 'No, I ain't
But I don't feel as well as I did.'

What do they have for lunch at the cannibal school?
*Human beans and boiled legs.*

Where is the best place to have a sick room?
Next to the school canteen.

SAM: What's wrong with school dinners?
FRED: Everything!

What looks like the Incredible Hulk?
*School dinners!*

Yesterday while eating school dinner, something very peculiar happened. Two of my potatoes came alive. There was a father and a girl. The girl said 'Dad, can I marry Dickie Davies?'

Dadtato: No!

Girltato: Why not?

Dadtato: Because he's a comantato!

PUPIL: Sir, can I pull the wishbone on the chicken?

TEACHER: Eat your dinner first.

PUPIL: But Sir, I was going to wish that I didn't have to!

ALAN: How did you get that medal?

BILLY: I saved the school.

ALAN: How did you do that?

BILLY: I shot the cooks.

'Cook, cook, will my hamburger be long?'
'No, boy, it'll be round.'

JOHN: Did I tell you about the three eggs we had for school dinner?

MOTHER: No.

JOHN: Two bad.

JOHN: I've got 2,000 bones in my body.

MOTHER: How come?

JOHN: I had fish for school dinner.

1ST BOY: I bet we'll have bread rolls tomorrow.

2ND BOY: I'll bring a cannon then.

'Cook, cook, this chicken has dots on.'
'That's alright, it's only chicken pox.'

PUPIL: I'll have a chop and chips, and make the chop lean!
DINNER LADY: Which way, left or right?

Two children were having their school dinner.
One said, 'What's that fly doing on your meat?'
The other replied, 'It probably died after tasting it!'

A boy came home from school and said to his mother, 'I was told off today at dinner.'
   'What for?'
   'The teacher said I'm greedy, I'm a slow finisher and I dribble too much.'
   'You must behave better than that. How are you getting on at football?'
   'The teacher said I'm greedy, I'm a slow finisher and I dribble too much.'

TOMMY: Miss, these rock cakes are too tough for me to chew.
MISS: Actually they are boiled potatoes.
TOMMY: Does that mean that this mop-like thing's a cabbage?

TEACHER: Why is this pie squashed?
BOY: Well you asked for a pie and step on it.

I never say school dinners are bad, but even the school dustbins have ulcers.

A portion of our school dinners is so small. They give us a magnifying glass with our knife and fork to make sure we can find it.

The meat is made of iron,
The spuds are made of steel,
And, if that don't get you,
The afters surely will!

Yesterday at school we had cottage pie; the council came round and condemned it.

A boy having school dinner goes up to the cook and says, 'Can I have some custard please?'
　'One lump or two?'

'The dinner lady's cooking Sunday lunch for us,' said Fred the newcomer.
　'Ugh, I suppose that means enthusiasm soup again, as always,' said Sid.
　'Enthusiasm soup – what's that?'
　'She puts everything she's got in it.'

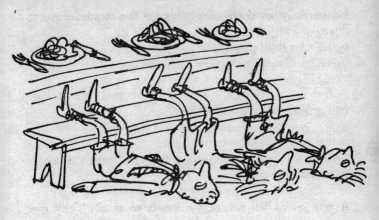

TEACHER: What is that going *yuk bump*, *yuk bump*, *yuk bump*?

PUPIL: The first-sitting people tasting the dinner and fainting.

The pigs refuse to eat
Our leftovers of peas and meat.
Of course I don't blame
'Cause I do the same
And chuck it under the seat.

If you stay to school dinners,
Better throw them aside.
A lot of kids didn't,
A lot of kids died.

The police cycling proficiency officer came to stay for dinner. We had I arrest stew.

The school dinners at our school are so cold that even the potatoes wear their jackets.

Dinner lady patrolling playground with shotgun.
Two ducks fly over.
DUCK 1: Quack, quack.
DUCK 2: I'm going as quack as I can.


A boy came out of the film club and said, 'I've seen a better film on the cook's gravy.'


PUPIL: Are slugs nice to eat, Sir?
TEACHER: Don't be so disgusting at the dinner table.
*After dinner.*
TEACHER: What was that you said about slugs?
PUPIL: You had one in your salad, but it's gone now.


MUM: You are going to have free school dinners.
JANE: I don't want three school dinners – I have a job eating one.


TEACHER (*to fat boy*): What's your favourite instrument?
BOY: The dinner bell, Sir.


BOY (*to cook*): We always have potatoes in their jackets, Miss – couldn't we have potatoes in their trousers instead?


Why are school dinners so good?
> *Because the top classes eat them.*

Why do the cooks dip their sponge fingers in paraffin?
> *To make them light of course.*

Why are school cooks cruel?
> *Because they beat eggs, whip cream and batter fish.*

Knock, knock.
Who's there?
Justin.
Justin who?
Justin time for dinner.

Knock, knock.
Who's there?
Doughnut.
Doughnut who?
Doughnut do that.

Knock, knock.
Who's there?
Egbert.
Egbert who?
Egbert no bacon.

Knock, knock.
Who's there?
William.
William who?
Williamake him some frogspawn pie!

What is a mushroom?
*The school dining hall.*

*Cheap Food* by Nora Bone
*The Biscuit Eater* by Martin Zempty
*Time to Eat* by Dean R. Bell
*School Dinners* by Jess Leavem
*School Dinners* by R. Revolting
*School Dinners* by Ivor Pain

Why is school custard lumpy?
*Because the cooks don't beat it enough.*

The other day we had frozen chicken for lunch. It wasn't meant to be frozen, but the dinner ladies put it in the fridge instead of the oven.

SCHOOL PIE EATING CONTEST

JOHN: My dinner was cold.
JAMES: How come?
JOHN: It was yesterday's.

JOHN: Miss, I eaten seven sausages for dinner.
TEACHER: Ate, John, ate.
JOHN: It may have been eight, Miss, I know I eaten an awful lot.

BOY: Our school cook really knows her modern technology and her history.
MUM: Does she?
BOY: Yes, today we had micro-chips in ancient grease.

TEACHER: Why are you the only child in the classroom today?
BILL: Because I was the only child who didn't have school dinner yesterday.

How did the dinner lady get an electric shock?
> *She stepped on a bun and a currant went up her leg.*

Why was the soup rich?
> *Because it had 14 carrots in it.*

BOY: I say, Miss, do you call this a three-course meal?
MISS: Yes, two chips and a pea.

A small boy was being served his dinner at the school canteen.

The dinner lady asked him, 'Would you like some meat?'

'Yes,' he said.

'Creamed potatoes or chips?'

'Yes,' he said.

'What's that little word you've forgotten?'

'Gravy,' he said.

JANE: Miss, this chop is very tough.
TEACHER: Yes, dear, it's probably a Karate chop.

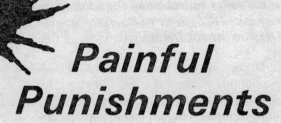

# Painful
# Punishments

## *Painful Punishments* by **Roald Dahl**

*Author of* Charlie and the Chocolate Factory *and many
other stories for both children and adults, Roald Dahl
was educated at St Peter's School, Weston-super-Mare,
and Repton School, Derbyshire.*

At my last boarding-school (age 13–18) there were at
least one hundred different diabolical punishments. But
that was more than fifty years ago and things have
changed a lot since then. We got punished for burning
the prefect's toast or if he found a speck of dust on a
shelf in his study, or for not touching the rims of our
straw hats as we passed a master on the road, or not
taking them off if we passed a master's wife. We got
punished for leaving games clothes on the floor of the
changing-room, for being late for anything at all, for
talking in class, or if the brass buttons on our O.T.C.
uniforms were not shining like gold.

Above all, we were punished for poor work. But the
master for whom one did the bad work never did the
punishing. That pleasure was reserved for one's
housemaster. A rather subtle method was employed by
which the form-master told the housemaster of your
misdemeanour. The form-master would say in class,
'Dahl, take eighty blue', or 'one hundred and twenty
blue' or whatever. 'Blue' was a special kind of blue
paper which only the housemaster possessed, and each
large page contained forty lines. You therefore had to go
to your housemaster to get it. After lunch every day,
there was a queue of boys in the housemaster's study
drawing out small fractions of their pocket-money

which they had deposited with him at the beginning of term. We always paid in £2 and drew it out in tiny little bits at a time – thruppence, sixpence or a shilling. A boy who had been given 'blue' would go to the end of this queue so that when his time came he would be alone with the housemaster. He would then be cross-examined, often beaten. Two hundred and forty blue, the maximum, was an automatic and severe thrashing. He would then have to go off and fill in all those two hundred and forty lines with an original composition of his own. Whatever other work he had to do or games he had to play, 'blue' had to be completed and delivered by hand to the form-master (often a mile away) before lock-up on that same day. Two-forty blue is three thousand words. That's quite a lot to do in your spare time in one afternoon. But do it you had to, and do it you did.

I only got two-forty blue once. That was from my German teacher. I hated German. I hated especially the way they twisted the sentences by putting the verbs at the end ('Will you a little piece of delicious new-baked bread have?'). Horrible. So I refused to work. So I got two-forty blue. So I got beaten. And I remember I wrote three thousand words by suppertime with a story called *The Life History of a Penny*.

May I add one thing. I don't see any harm in whacking boys for being lazy. One has to work so *hard* later on in life that the sooner one acquires the habit the better, and if a good whacking's going to help, then okay. It helped me.

JOHNNY: Teacher, would you cane someone for something they didn't do?

TEACHER: Of course not, Johnny.

JOHNNY: Good, because I haven't done my homework.

TEACHER: Hold out your hand, Jones. I'm going to give you the cane.

JONES: Oh, thank you, Sir – what shall I do with it?

BOY: What did you get from the head teacher, Jim?

JIM: A red star.

BOY: I thought he was going to cane you.

JIM: He did. He put a red star on my bottom.

What is dangerous and sits in the corner of the room?
*The teacher's cane.*

'I believe in getting to the bottom of things,' said the headmaster as he caned the naughty boy.

Why do teachers use a bamboo cane?
*Because when the cane goes 'bam' the child goes 'boo'.*

'Doctor, doctor, I've just been caned, and I can't stand it any longer!'
'Well, sit down then.'

Why do teachers use cane?
*Because they have no lumps.*

BILL: I'm not looking forward to going into Mr Jones's class.
BEN: Why not?
BILL: My father says that he's a big *strapping* man.

Knock, knock.
Who's there?
Ivor.
Ivor who?
Ive 'ad a caning, so let me in!

49

Knock, knock.
Who's there?
Anna.
Anna who?
Anna 'nother caning!

There was an old teacher called Green,
Who invented a caning machine.
On the 99th stroke
The rotten thing broke
And hit poor Green on the beam!

*Discipline* by I. Flogham
*Punishment and Discipline* by Ben Dover
*Who to Cane* by E. Z. E. Didit
*How to Get into Trouble* by Nick N. Apple
*I'm in Trouble* by C. Lee-Boy

How did the boy feel after being caned?
    *Absolutely whacked.*

JANE: What steps do you take when you see a teacher
  with a cane?
JULIE: Big ones!

One day a boy came home from school and his Dad said:
'You've been sent home, haven't you?'
  'Yes.'
  'What for?'
  'The lad sitting next to me was smoking.'
  'Well what did they send you home for?'
  'It was me that set him on fire.'

Why didn't the teacher give the naughty boy the cane?
>     *Because he didn't have one.*

What did the Cane say to his brother?
>     '*Are you Abel?*'

What do you do when you have the cane?
>     *Put a book down your trousers.*

Why did the boy like getting the cane?
>     *So he could feed his pet panda.*

TEACHER: If you can show me a dirtier hand than yours
  I won't cane you!
BOY: Take a look at my other hand, Sir.

Why did the cane become stuck?
>     *Because it was a stick.*

Why can't teachers smack children with rulers?
>     *Because Mrs Thatcher is too heavy.*

A boy's punishment for disobedience was to write a 100-
word essay. He wrote *Mrs Smith went outside and called
for her cat, 'Here Pussy, Pussy, Pussy ...'* (and so on for
100 words)!

What do the letter 'K' and children have in common?
*They're both on the end of the stick.*

What happens if you draw on the blackboard and the teacher told you not to?
*She draws a smack.*

What takes hundreds of lickings from a teacher?
*A lolly.*

HEADMASTER: Right, Jim, do you want the belt?
JIM: No, I've already got one.

TEACHER: David, write out 'I must not forget' 100 times.
DAVID: But Sir, I only forgot it twice.

What's the best attended class at school?
    *Detention class.*

A little girl kept writing 'I gone home', instead of 'I went home', so the teacher told the girl to write 'I went home' fifty times, after school. When the girl had finished she left a note for the teacher, 'I done my lines and I gone home.'

TEACHER (*to child in detention*): This is the fifth time this week that you have been kept in. What have you to say for yourself?
CHILD: Thank goodness it's Saturday tomorrow.

At assembly a headmaster made an announcement to the schoolchildren: 'From now on there will be no physical punishment at this school.'
    A hand shot up. 'Sir, does that mean we have to bring sandwiches?'

Our school doesn't give detention as a punishment, they give us a second helping of school dinners instead.

TEACHER: Write *I must not punch girls in the mouth* 100 times.
BILL: Yes, Sir. (writes) *I must not punch girls in the mouth 100 times. I must not punch girls in the mouth 100 times.*

53

HEADMASTER: What punishment do you think I should give?

BOY: I've already had some punishment looking at your face.

TEACHER: You have been talking all lesson; do fifty lines. (Gives boy a plain sheet of paper.)

TEACHER (*later*): Where are the lines I asked you to do?

BOY: There were none on the paper, miss.

An inspector was passing along a school corridor when he heard a lot of noise from one of the classrooms. He hurried into the room and said, 'Will that noisy boy stand in the corner? Now, where's your teacher?'

'In the corner,' said the class.

TEACHER (*to a child who is making a lot of unnecessary noise*): If you keep on behaving like this you'll have the strap.

CHILD: What are the other prizes, Miss?

'Teacher, teacher, what big hands you have.'
'All the better to smack you with.'

# Excruciating Exams

## *Excruciating Exams* by Sally James

*Tiswas trouble-shooter and custard-pie-chucker, Sally James attended Hinckley Wood Primary School, Gladys Dare Stage School and the Arts Education Trust.*

I have spent many hours of my life taking exams. I went to a stage school, where I spent half the day learning academic subjects and the rest of the time on dancing, drama and similar things. Apart from all the normal

academic exams, we also had to take ballet, modern dance, speech, drama, tap and even ballroom dancing. You never knew when you might be called upon for the odd quick-step – and the way I do the quick-step is *very* odd. At my school there were 35 girls to every boy ('Lucky old boys!' I hear you mutter) so in ballroom dancing half the girls had to dance the men's part. I was one of these unfortunates and to this day insist on steering my partner around as I did at school.

About the only thing we did not take exams in was singing, but those of you who have heard my performance of the *Bucket of Water Song* will agree I would have passed with flying colours!!

Because we had to squash all our ordinary academic education into half a day and at the end of the course sit O-levels, we had regular exams to prepare us and keep us up to scratch. Our history teacher went one better and gave us a good grilling every Monday morning. The thought of that completely ruined any idea we might have had of enjoying our weekends. Fortunately I was quite good at history, so I became the popular girl to sit

next to every Monday – well, it was useful for bribing sweets out of people! And of course all the pommelling of dates into my head has proved extremely useful in my chosen career as a bucket-bunger and custard-pie-chucker.

When I left school I thought I'd put all those exams behind me but then I had to face the most gruelling of all – The Driving Test! I got off to a great start – the handbag I was carrying had a very long strap which I succeeded in tangling around the gear-stick. When something like that happens it's no good joking with the examiner – they are specially trained not to laugh or even to speak – it's a miracle they breathe! Anyway, my driving skill pulled me through – or was it the fact that I was wearing an extremely short mini-skirt? Perhaps the examiner was human after all?

FATHER: Well, Son, how are your exam marks?
SON: They're under water.
FATHER: What do you mean?
SON: Below 'C' level.

1ST MUM: What's your son going to be when he passes all his exams?
2ND MUM: A pensioner.

'Exams, exams, exams, I wonder what they're for?
Exams are made to teach us pupils, but we
think it's a terrible bore.'

*Some answers given in the history examination:*
1 The Normans went through the town in 1066 and that was a pretty fast time for those days.
2 King Alfred was called the Grate because that's where he burned the cakes.
3 The Peelers were the followers of William of Orange.

After the history examination the teacher spoke to the form:
'I'm very disappointed with many of you because you weren't concentrating on your work. I asked what happened after the Saxons had beaten the Vikings at Stamford Bridge, and most of you wrote that they were "knocked out in the semi-final".'

What's black and white and difficult?
*An exam paper.*

Did you hear about the horse in the classroom?
*He was taking his hay levels.*

EXAM QUESTION: What does 1066 mean to you?
ANSWER: William the Conqueror's phone number.

Tommy was finishing his prayers: 'God bless my mother and my father, and please make Montreal the Capital of Canada.'

'Why Tommy!' exclaimed his mother. 'Why did you say that?'

'Well,' explained Tommy, 'I wrote that on my exam paper.'

Janet looked very pleased as she came into the house after school:

JANET: Mummy, I won the nature study prize.

MOTHER: How lovely. How did you do it?

JANET: Teacher asked the class how many legs an ostrich has, and I said three.

MOTHER: But it has two legs.

JANET: I was the nearest.

DAD: Well, did you get a good place in your exam?
SON: Yes Dad, I sat next to the radiator.

TOM: Dad, I've got good news.
DAD: Have you passed your exams?
TOM: No, not exactly, but I was top of those who failed.

'How did you get on in the maths exams?'
'I only got one sum wrong.'
'That's very good. How many were there?'
'Twelve.'
'Twelve? So you got eleven of the sums right!'
'No – they were the ones I couldn't do!'


TEACHER: Jason, did you miss maths today?
JASON: No, Miss, not a bit.

TEACHER: How does it happen, do you suppose, that
you have exactly the same answers as Katie in the maths
test?
PUPIL: Because we used the same pencil.

TEACHER: Melvin, you copied from Paul's paper, didn't
you?
MELVIN: How did you find out?
TEACHER: His paper says 'I don't know' and yours says
'Me neither'!

TEACHER: How do you think you are going to get up
to A-level standard?
PUPIL: With a lift, Miss.

TEACHER: Jimmy, why do you always fail your exams?
JIMMY: Because I always get the wrong exam paper.

TEACHER: I thought I told you not to look in your bag. You could have the answers.
PUPIL: I'm not, Sir, I'm looking in Paul's bag – he's got the answers.

TEACHER: Everybody has to take an exam.
PUPIL: But I don't like eggs'n'ham.

TEACHER: Never mind today's date, Peter. Get on with your answers.
PETER: Well, I wanted to have *something* right on my paper.

'Teacher, Teacher, how many sums did I get out of 50?'
'All of them, except 49.'

GIRL: Why do we have to do exams?
TEACHER: If you do well, it's a shining example of how bright you are.
GIRL: Sounds as if I'd better take my torch with me, then I won't get confused.

TEACHER: In the exam you will be allowed half an hour for each question.
PUPIL: How long for the answer, Sir?

This chap went in for an exam, and the teacher asked when he had had his last exam.
   '1945.'
   The teacher said, 'That's a long time ago.'
   The chap said, 'No, it's only 2015 now.'

PUPIL: I had one hundred and one in my exam.
TEACHER: You couldn't have, it's out of a hundred.
PUPIL: I know, I had one hundred per cent and won.

After an examination the teacher said to a boy, 'On your paper you have written against many of the questions, "See Simon Jones's paper."'

'Yes, Sir. I thought you didn't want us to copy.'

Who scored best in the animal exam?
> *The cheetah.*

Knock, knock.
Who's there?
Exam.
Exam who?
Eggs, ham and cheese.

Knock, knock.
Who's there?
Sammy.
Sammy who?
Sammyxams we've got to do.

Roses are red,
Violets are blue.
I copied your exams,
And I failed too.

*Good Exam Results* by B. O. Nick Brain
*How to Cheat in Exams* by P. King
*How to Pass Exams* by Vic Tree

EXAM QUESTION: Why were the early days called the Dark Ages?
ANSWER: Because there were so many knights.

In the exams a teacher asked a boy where Turkey was.
'Eaten last Christmas,' came the reply.

MUSIC EXAMINER: Is there anything special you'd like to play?
PUPIL: Yes Miss, truant.

EXAM QUESTION: In Great Britain, where are the kings and queens usually crowned?
ANSWER: On the head!

1ST BOY: I'm studying Ancient History.
2ND BOY: So am I.
1ST BOY: Let's go and talk over old times.

An R.E. teacher did not know how to mark exams.
    'Here, try this,' said the woodwork teacher, giving him a spirit level.

BOY: How were your exam questions?
GIRL: The questions were easy – but I had trouble with the answers.

Two girls were talking about their end-of-year exams:
'On my report I got ITV, BBC for French.'
'ITV, BBC – what does that mean?'
'Intonation Terribly Vague, But Becoming Clearer.'

What exams does Santa Claus take?
*Ho! Ho! Ho! Levels.*

EXAM QUESTION: Who invented arithmetic?
ANSWER: Henry VIII (Henry the $\frac{1}{8}$).

How do they mark exams in the Communist world?
*You get Marx out of ten.*

EXAM QUESTION: Who was the world's greatest thief?
ANSWER: Atlas, because he held up the whole world.

Why is an optician like a teacher?
*They both test the pupils.*

EXAM QUESTION: After the Glorious Revolution, which king and queen ruled jointly?
ANSWER: Ethel Bert.

EXAMINER: What can you tell me about the Dead Sea?
JOHN: I didn't even know it was ill.

# Terrific
# Teachers

## *Terrific Teachers* by Roger McGough

*Roger McGough is a poet and playwright. His schools were Star of the Sea Infants' School, Seaforth, and St Mary's College, Liverpool.*

Imagine a dragon: fierce, with yellow fangs and evil-smelling breath; bulging eyes and green scaly skin. If you can imagine that dragon with nail varnish on its claws, wearing a brown tweed suit and ginger hair tied up in a bun, then you can imagine Miss Bolger.

Miss Bolger, the scourge of Junior 2, Terror of the Tongue, Attila the Bun. She was a sorceress who could turn a classroom into a torture chamber and with a wave of her magic cane turn thirty infants into quivering jellies. She taught us the three Ss – sweating, stammering and skins (how to jump out of).

In complete contrast was Miss Davis, a dear, gentle old soul, who loved us all, even the lowliest and smelliest (even Lacey). Her lessons came gift-wrapped, because the reward for a correct answer would often be a sweet and for everyone there was a smile and a word of encouragement.

We repaid her kindness by occasionally locking her in the bookroom, and putting cockroaches in her spectacle case.

As I grew older, my legs grew shorter and my trousers longer, so I went to grammar school, where most of the schoolmasters were men. Here, the good, the bad, and the ugly swept through classrooms breathing not fire, but vulgar fractions, Latin verbs and laws of physics. Great gollups of information which passed through my brain like steam through a football net.

To help liven up the lessons, they used black leather straps and how well I remember lazy summer afternoons, the droning of bees outside, the lilt of the strap and the howling of little boys within. We gave them nicknames: 'The Last Count' (always out before the bell), 'The Tooleater' ($3\frac{1}{2}$ pints every lunchtime ... i.e., the two-litre), and 'Rumblintum'.

There was one particular thug I remember with affection, who, as well as being President of the N.S.P.C.C. (National Society for the Promotion of Cruelty to Children) was the gym master. S.A.S.-trained, his hobbies were shouting and bruising, and woe betide any boy who forgot his pumps or put his underpants on back to front (or vice versa). But even though his brain was muscle-bound, he had a nice sense of humour and would always laugh heartily if somebody fell off the wall-bars or dropped a bench on their toe.

But, like everyone else, I survived and as I grew older I got to know and to like many of those whom at first I believed came from Outer Space. Teachers, those strange beings who live on the other side of the blackboard. Who eat chalk and talk in loud riddles.

Some nights I wake up sweating after a nightmare, in which I had to lie to attention for two hours and not make a sound. On waking, I realize Miss Bolger had been in charge of my sleep. Of course, she's hung up her cane, and long since departed this life. But I bet she's still bossing kids around somewhere. Miss Bolger, now in Paradise Junior School, making the infant angels cross their wings and sit up straight. Putting the fear of God into them. It must be hell.

TEACHER: What do you think you are doing, crawling into school ten minutes late?

PUPIL: You told me never to walk into school ten minutes late!

TEACHER: Peter, where were you yesterday?

PETER: I went for a haircut, Sir.

TEACHER: What! In school time?

PETER: But Sir, it grew in school time.

TEACHER: Not all of it.

PETER: But I didn't have all of it off, Sir.

TEACHER: You missed school yesterday, didn't you Tommy?

TOMMY: Yes, Sir. Next time I'll aim properly!

TEACHER: Smith, now that you've kindly consented to come to school, what would you like to do?

SMITH: Go home.

TEACHER: Why are you so late?

PUPIL: Well, I was obeying that sign saying 'school ahead, go slow'.

TEACHER: You're late this morning.

BOY: I know, I got stuck in the jam.

TEACHER: Why were you late this morning?

PUPIL: Because I squeezed the toothpaste too hard, and it took me half an hour to get the paste back in the tube.

TEACHER (*on phone*): You said Jimmy has a cold and can't come to school? To whom am I speaking?

VOICE: This is my father.

TEACHER: You missed school yesterday, didn't you?
BOY: Not a bit.


When a teacher entered her classroom, she noticed a little pool of water near the blackboard.

'Who is responsible for this?' she asked. There was a deathly hush. 'I want whoever did this to own up. We will all close our eyes and then the guilty boy must come forward and write his name on the blackboard.'

Everybody closed eyes obediently and presently there were furtive footsteps up to the blackboard, a little pause and then the sound of chalk on the board, followed by the retreating steps of the writer.

When the command was given for all to open their eyes, it was seen that there was another little puddle of water by the first, while on the blackboard was the message, 'The Phantom Piddler Strikes Again!'


TEACHER: If you keep on getting things wrong, Jones, I don't see much of a future for you.
JONES: Don't worry, Sir, I want to be a weather forecaster.


TEACHER: Johnson, didn't you hear me call you?
JOHNSON: Yes, Sir, but you told us not to answer back.


TEACHER: Do you want a pocket calculator?
PUPIL: No, thank you, I know how many pockets I've got.


A boy sat in the classroom chewing. The teacher said to him, 'You were eating peanuts in class on Monday, caramels on Tuesday, now you're chewing treacle toffee. Why?'

'Please Miss, I couldn't get any jelly babies.'

TEACHER: What are you reading?
PUPIL: I dunno.
TEACHER: But you're reading aloud.
PUPIL: But I'm not listening.

ALEC (*reading*): 'I was going there tomorrow ...'
TEACHER: Alec! Watch your tense.
ALEC: What do I want with tents? I'm not going camping.

TEACHER: I saw you stealing a plum from outside the greengrocer's, but I was pleased to see you put it straight back. Did you hear your conscience telling you it was wrong?'
ALFIE: No Sir, I saw a maggot.

TEACHER: Billy, please do not whistle while you are studying.
BILLY: Oh, I'm not studying – I'm just whistling.

TEACHER (*to pupil*): How many million trillion times have I told you not to exaggerate?

TEACHER: Who let the air out of the bus wheel?
PUPIL: The nail did, Sir.

TEACHER: What would you say if I came in to school with a face like yours?
MATTHEW: I'd be too polite to mention it.

TEACHER: Were you copying his sums?
MARK: No Sir, just looking to see if he got mine right.

TEACHER: Will you please pay a little attention, class.
CLASS: We are, Miss. As little as possible.

TEACHER: Now Herbert, you must learn to give and take.
HERBERT: But I did give and take. I gave him a black eye, and took his apple.

TEACHER: Stop showing off, William. Do you think that you're the teacher here?
WILLIAM: No, Sir.
TEACHER: Then stop acting like a fool!

TEACHER: Order, children, order!
BILL: I'll have jelly and custard.

TEACHER: When do you like school best?
PUPIL: When it's closed.

TEACHER: Billy, I hope I didn't see you copying from David's work.
BILLY: I hope you didn't, too.

TEACHER: Tommy, put some more water in the fish tank.
TOMMY: Why, Miss, I only put some in yesterday, and he hasn't drunk that yet.

TEACHER: Did the bee sting you?
PHILIP: Yes, Sir.
TEACHER: Put some cream on it.
PHILIP: Don't be mad, Sir, it'll be miles away.

Why was the headmaster worried?
>*Because there were too many rulers in school.*

TEACHER: Can you see these sums?
BOY: No.
TEACHER: Have your eyes been checked?
BOY: No, they've always been blue.

TEACHER: What is this picture of?
BOY: Don't know.
TEACHER: It's a kangaroo.
BOY: What's a kangaroo, Miss?
TEACHER: It's a native of Australia.
BOY: Cor – my big sister's married one of them.

VICTORIAN SCHOOLMASTER: Switzerland is as big as Siam. Now, Basil, are you listening? How big is Switzerland?
BASIL: As big as you are, Sir.

What is the difference between a lazy teacher and an angler?
>*One hates his books and the other baits his hooks.*

JIM: Father says that I'm slow but sure.
TEACHER: That's true! Slow to learn but sure to forget.

What is the difference between an engine driver and a schoolmaster?
*One minds the train and the other trains the mind.*

'Teacher, teacher, I think I'm invisible.'
'Who said that?'

BOY: Miss, how do you spell Llewellyn?
TEACHER: Llewellyn, L l e w e l l y n.
BOY: Well the boy next door spells his name like this: L l e w e l y n.
TEACHER: Well, boy, that makes one L of a difference.

'Now children,' said the teacher, 'there's a wonderful example for us in the life of the ant. Every day the ant goes to work. Every day the ant is busy. And in the end, what happens?'

A voice came from the back of the room, 'Somebody steps on him.'

PUPIL: Tin can, empty bottle, paper bag ...
TEACHER: Stop talking rubbish.

SCIENCE TEACHER: How do you know that carrots are
good for your eyes?
PUPIL: I've never seen a rabbit wearing glasses, Miss.

My teacher has turned into a bat. She keeps hanging
  around me!

The school inspector asked the class to tell him a number.
  '27,' called out one pupil, and the inspector wrote down
72 on the blackboard. No one said anything, so again he
asked the class for a number.
  '24,' came a voice and again the inspector wrote on the
blackboard, 42. And again no one said a word.
  'Can I have another number, please?' asked the inspector.
  '33,' shouted someone, and a quiet voice in the back
added 'Lets see 'im muck abaht wiv 'at one!'

TEACHER: In which part of the world are people most
  ignorant?
JACK: London.
TEACHER: Why do you say that?
JACK: The geography books say that's where the popu-
  lation is most dense.

The Sunday school teacher wasn't getting much response
from her pupils. 'Doesn't anyone know who Peter was?'
  A small voice from the back piped up, 'Wasn't he a
wabbit?'

TEACHER: Give me a sentence with the words *defence*,
  *defeat* and *detail* in it.
ANDREW: When a horse jumps over defence, defeat go
  before detail!

What type of feet does a maths teacher have?
    *Square feet.*

TEACHER: If I had ten flies on my desk, and killed one, how many would I have left?
PUPIL: One, the others would fly away.

TEACHER: If you take 7.3 plus 9.8 from 11.80189 times 7.9999, what do you get?
JACK: The wrong answer.

'There are five fingers on one hand and five fingers on the other. If three fingers were missing, what would you have?'
'No more music lessons.'

TEACHER: If you had five apples on your desk and the boy next to you took three, what would you have?
BOY: A scrap, Miss.

BOY: Do you know that the most intelligent person in the world has gone deaf?
TEACHER: No!
BOY: Pardon?

BOY: What's the difference between wages and salaries?
TEACHER: If you get a wage, you get paid once a week. If you get a salary, you get paid once a month. For example, I get a salary. I am paid once a month.
BOY: Please, Sir, where do you work?

'Teacher! Teacher! Why do you call me Pilgrim?'
'Because you're making a little progress.'

JOHNNY: Miss, I ain't got a pencil.
TEACHER: No, Johnny, not 'ain't'. I haven't got a pencil! They haven't got a pencil! You haven't got a pencil!
JOHNNY: Gosh, what happened to all the pencils?

'Teacher! Teacher! Why do you keep me in this cage?'
'Because you're the teacher's pet.'

'Teacher! Teacher! My knees keep knocking.'
'Well, tie some cymbals to them, and join the school band.'

'My teacher's got a new car.'
'What make is it?'
'It's a Rolls Canardly.'
'Never heard of it.'
'Haven't you? It rolls down one hill and can 'ardly get up the next.'

TOM: Sometimes I like teachers.
BILL: When?
TOM: When they are at home.

JOHNNY: Miss, who is teacher's pet?
TEACHER: My dog.

Two girls were discussing the history teacher. 'She really knows what happened in the nineteenth century, doesn't she?'

'She ought to,' said the other, 'she was there for most of it.'

'How did Hangman get its name?'
'You hang your teacher when you win ...'
'But how do you know when you've won?'
'The teacher screams.'

FRED: Why do you call your teacher Treasure?
JOE: Because we wonder where she was dug up.

BOY: Miss, my pen's run out.
TEACHER: Well, go and get it then.

PUPIL: I don't think I deserved the 0% you gave me.
TEACHER: Neither do I but it's the lowest I could give you.

GIRL: My teacher's a peach.
BOY: You mean she's sweet?
GIRL: No, she has a heart of stone.

PUPIL: If athletes get athlete's foot, what do astronauts get?
TEACHER: Missile toe!

CHILD (*in nursery*): Please Miss, my fumb hurts. I jammed it in the door.
TEACHER: Oh dear; you mustn't say 'fumb', it's th … th … thumb.
CHILD: But please, Miss … my … th … thinger hurts too.

BILLY: Teacher, teacher, can you help me out?
TEACHER: Certainly, which way did you come in?

What did the teacher bee say to the naughty bee?
    '*Behive yourself*.'

TEACHER: What is a comet?
CLARA: A star with a tail.
TEACHER: Name one.
CLARA: Lassie.

1ST BOY: I wish we could sell our teachers.
2ND BOY: Why?
1ST BOY: Because I read that at auctions Old Masters are fetching big prices.

What did the teacher say to the skeleton?
*'I've got a bone to pick with you.'*

TEACHER: David, what is the oldest plant?
DAVID: Thyme!

TEACHER: What bird cannot fly, but has wings?
PUPIL: A roast chicken, Sir.

TEACHER: Can anyone tell me what sort of animal a slug is?

DENIS: It's a snail with a housing problem.

TEACHER: What do we make from horn?

PUPIL: Hornaments, Sir.

TEACHER: When the animals came into Noah's Ark, they all came in pairs.

JOHNNY: That's not true. The worms came in apples.

TEACHER: Now, Doreen, what do we call the outer part of a tree?

DOREEN: Don't know, Miss.

TEACHER: Bark, you silly girl, bark.

DOREEN: Woof woof.

TEACHER: What is electrical on a telegraph pole?

PUPIL: Why-er ...

TEACHER: Correct.

TEACHER: Where can you find giant snails?

BOY: At the end of giants' fingers.

TEACHER: What happens to gold when it's exposed to the air?

BOY: It's stolen, Sir.

TEACHER: What followed the dinosaur?
PUPIL: Its tail.

TEACHER: Class, can anybody tell me something that sees better than a boy?
ALEC: An eagle, Sir.
TEACHER: Very good. And something that hears better than a boy?
ALEC: A dog, Sir.
TEACHER: Excellent! And something that smells better than a boy?
ALEC: A rose, Sir!

TEACHER: Why do animals have fur coats?
DUNCE: Because they'd look silly in plastic macs, Sir.

TEACHER: Light travels at 186,000 miles per second. Don't you think that's remarkable?
PUPIL: Not really; it's downhill all the way.

TEACHER: Johnny, could you tell me something about Einstein's Theory of Relativity?
JOHNNY: Well there was Grandma and Grandad Einstein, Mr and Mrs Einstein and their son Albert ...

TEACHER: What is the fastest thing in the water?
BOY: A motor pike.

BOTANY TEACHER: Tell me something about the mint plant.
PUPIL: It makes money.

TEACHER: To what family does the walrus belong?
PUPIL: I don't know. No family in our street has one.

MUSIC TEACHER: How do you grow musical flowers?
CHILD: I don't know, how do you grow musical flowers?
MUSIC TEACHER: With Yehudi manure!

ANDREW: Did the music teacher really say your voice was
   out of this world?
PETER: Not exactly. She said it was unearthly.

GEORGE: Did you hear about the music teacher?
MARK: No.
GEORGE: He thought a humbug was a flea singing.

ART MASTER: Patricia, I told you to draw a horse and cart, but you've only drawn the horse.
PATRICIA: Yes, Sir, the horse will draw the cart.

TEACHER: Tell me, as precisely as possible, all you know about the great English water-colour painters of the eighteenth century.
PUPIL: They're all dead.

Our art teacher is always grumbling so we call her the Mona Lisa.

WOODWORK TEACHER: What's that you're making, James?
BOY: It's a portable, Sir.
TEACHER: A portable what?
BOY: I don't know yet, I've only made the handles.

WOODWORK MASTER (*holding up a piece of sandpaper*):
What is this I am holding?
PUPIL: A map of the Sahara desert.

'I don't think my woodwork teacher likes me ... He's teaching me how to make a coffin.'

TEACHER: Why did Stone Age man draw pictures of hippopotamuses and rhinoceroses on cave walls?
BOY: Because he didn't know how to spell them.

TEACHER: Who was Shakespeare?
ALEC: A corset manufacturer ...
TEACHER: Wherever did you get that idea?
ALEC: Well, wasn't he the one who wrote, 'I'll put a girdle round the earth in forty minutes?'

TEACHER: Can anybody tell me something about Christopher Columbus?
DESMOND: He discovered America was very economical.
TEACHER: How do you mean economical, Desmond?
DESMOND: He was the only man to travel 3,000 miles on a galleon.

TEACHER: When was Rome built?
ANDREW: At night.
TEACHER: What makes you think that?
ANDREW: I've heard that Rome wasn't built in a day.

TEACHER: Who invented underground tunnels?
BOY: Moles, Miss.

TEACHER: Albert, who were the Phoenicians?
ALBERT: The people who invented Phoenician blinds.

TEACHER: Millie, spell *mouse*.
MILLIE: M-O-U-S.
TEACHER: But what's at the end of it.
MILLIE: A tail.

TEACHER: What do you call a cow's skin?
JIMMY: Dunno, Sir.
TEACHER: HIDE, my boy, HIDE.
JIMMY: Quick, lads, under the table!

TEACHER: Martha, what does the word *trickle* mean?'
MARTHA: To run slowly.
TEACHER: Quite right. And what does the word *anecdote* mean?
MARTHA: A short funny tale.
TEACHER: Right again. Now can you give me a sentence with both those words in it?
MARTHA: Er – our dog trickled down the street wagging his anecdote!

TEACHER: John, what is a cannibal?
JOHN: I don't know.
TEACHER: Well, if you ate your mother and father, what would you be then?
JOHN: An orphan.

TEACHER: Jimmy, have you been listening?
JIMMY: Yes, Miss.
TEACHER: What is an owl?
JIMMY: Someone in pain, Miss.

TEACHER: Now Tommy, give me a sentence with the word *centimetre* in it.
TOMMY: Er – my auntie was coming from the station and I was centimetre.

TEACHER: Simon, can you spell your name backwards?

SIMON: No Mis.

TEACHER: Tom, make up a sentence using the word *lettuce*.

TOM: Let us out of school early.

TEACHER: Martin, how do you spell *crocodile*?

MARTIN: K R O K O D I L.

TEACHER: The dictionary spells it C R O C O D I L E.

MARTIN: But, Sir, you asked me how *I* spell it, not how the dictionary spells it.

TEACHER: Can anyone tell me what is the meaning of the word *dogma*?

BOY: The mother of some pups, Miss.

TEACHER: The word *politics* – give me an example of how to use it.

MANDY: My parrot swallowed a watch, and now Polly ticks.

GEOGRAPHY TEACHER: Did you ever see the Catskill Mountains?
SMALL SAM: No, but I've seen them kill mice.

Our geography teacher is so bad, he got lost showing some parents around the school.

TEACHER: Mark, where does your mum come from?
MARK: Alaska.
TEACHER: Don't bother, I'll ask her myself.

TEACHER: If mud makes bricks and bricks make walls, what do walls make?
SALLY: Icecream.

TEACHER: What is the most common phrase in school?
BOY: I don't know.
TEACHER: Correct.

TEACHER: How old are you?
SMALL CHILD: I'm not old. I'm nearly new.

TEACHER: How do fishermen make their nets?
BOB: Easily – they just take a lot of holes and sew them together.

TEACHER: John, what is the Order of the Bath?
JOHN: Dad, Mum, my sister and then me.

TEACHER: And what might your name be, little man?
NEW BOY: It might be Cedric, but it ain't.

TEACHER: How old are you, Mark?
MARK: Nine, Sir.
TEACHER: And what are you going to be?
MARK: Ten, Sir.

TEACHER (*to pupil*): No Wilkins, BC does not mean Before
Calculators.

There were three boys. One was a new boy, and the other
two had been at school for two years. When they got to
school the teacher said, 'Why are you so late?'

The boys replied, 'We've been so busy throwing
peanuts into the river that we forgot the time.'

Just then, the new boy walked in, soaking wet.

'Ah, a new boy,' teacher exclaimed. 'What's your name?'

'Peanuts, Sir.'

When a teacher told his class to write the longest sentence
they could compose, a bright spark wrote, 'Imprisonment
for life!'

*Teachers* by R. Hopeless
*What Teachers Have to Go Through* by Ruth Lesschild
*How to Treat a Pupil* by I. Knowhow
*What Do Children Do at School?* by Driveyer Roundthe-
   bend
*The Big Book of Knowledge* by I. Dunnoe and Noah Little

Knock, knock.
Who's there?
R. Tea.
R. Tea who? (I know, Ahh, tea and biscuits.)
No, our teacher's coming.

Kick, kick.
Who's there?
Teacher.
Teacher who?
Teach yer to fix a knocker.

There was a fat teacher called Bet,
Who sat in the classroom and ate.
She spent all her cash on bangers and mash
And ended up with a £90 debt.

A mouse woke a teacher, Miss Dowd.
She was frightened and screamed very loud.
Then a happy thought hit her
To scare off the critter –
She sat up in bed and miaowed.

Our school is a good wee school –
It's made of brick and plaster.
The only thing that's wrong with it
Is the bald-headed headmaster!

There was a teacher called Mohammed Ben Ali
Ben Tonki,
Who went for a ride on a donkey.
Then it suddenly spoke
(This miraculous moke)
Saying, 'Get off and walk, I feel wonkey.'

There was a young teacher from Harrow,
Whose nose was too long and too narrow.
It gave so much trouble,
That he bent it up double
And wheeled it round school in a barrow.

Build a bonfire,
Build a bonfire,
Put the teachers at the top.
Put the prefects in the middle
And we'll burn the whole lot.

There was an old teacher, McGees,
Who thought he was going to sneeze.
The class said, 'Achoo',
McGees caught the flu
And blew all the class into trees!

There once was a teacher called Leach
Who took us all to the beach.
It said on a sign
'Watch out for the mine' –
The last thing we heard was his screech.

HEADMASTER: Did you break that window?
BOY: No, Sir, my ball did.

There once was a teacher from Leeds
Who swallowed a packet of seeds.
In less than an hour
Her nose was a flower
And her hair was a
    bunch of weeds.

Why is a schoolmistress like the letter C?
*Because she forms lasses into classes.*

When is a schoolmaster like a man with one eye?
*When he has a vacancy for a pupil.*

The boy said to the headmaster, 'I was at the zoo during my holidays.'

The headmaster said, 'So was I.'

To which the boy replied, 'I didn't see you there. Which cage were you in?'

HEADMASTER: Mrs Smith, I'm proud of your teaching and your class work. How do you manage to keep on your toes with such lively children?

TEACHER: They put drawing pins on my chair.

HEADMASTER: What do you mean by coming to school drunk, Jane?

TEACHER: Sorry, Head, I've been at the Teacher's all night.

The headmaster said that after assembly there would be a hymn practice for the boys. Someone asked if there would be a her practice for the girls.

FATHER: Well Johnny, do you think your new teacher likes you?

JOHNNY: Oh yes, she keeps putting little wee kisses by my sums.

FATHER: I'm not pleased with your end of term report, son.

SON: Neither was my teacher, but he insisted on sending it.

MUM: Why are you taking your toy car to school?

BOY: To drive my teacher up the wall.

'Now then, Billy,' said his teacher, 'who knocked down the walls of Jericho?'

'I didn't do it!' said Billy and went home crying.

At home Billy's dad asked why he was crying.

'The teacher accused me of knocking down the walls of Jericho and I didn't do it.'

So Billy's dad phoned up the teacher to tell him that he was going to report him. The Education Committee phoned up the teacher.

'Listen, if Billy says he didn't do it, he didn't, but if you can't find the culprit who did, we'll pay for any damage.'

SISTER: Andrew, why are you going to school in a cowboy suit?
ANDREW: Our teacher is teaching us to draw.

BOY: My teacher does bird imitations.
MUM: Really?
BOY: She watches me like a hawk.

Boy arrives home covered in spots.
'Mam, teacher sent me home.
I think she said I've got decimals.'

A girl said to her father, 'Our teacher was telling us today about the Battle of Waterloo.'
'What did he say?'
'He was lucky, he escaped with just a flesh wound.'

LITTLE GIRL: Mummy, teacher was asking me today if I had any brothers and sisters.
MOTHER: That's nice dear, and what did she say when you told her you were an only child?
LITTLE GIRL: Oh she just said, 'Thank goodness.'

BOB: Teacher says that I'm like Cromwell, Lincoln and Napoleon.
FATHER: Really. Why?
BOB: Well, I went down in history.

Why did the teacher go to the optician?
*Because he had bad pupils.*

Why did the teacher put on the lights?
*Because the class was so dim.*

When a teacher closes his eyes, why should it remind him of an empty classroom?
*Because there are no pupils to see.*

Did you hear about the cross-eyed teacher?
*She couldn't control her pupils.*

Why did the teacher wear dark glasses?
*Because her class was so bright.*

Teacher was astounded and said to the boy that it was unbelievable that he lived so close to a river and yet he couldn't swim.
'There's lots of air and I can't fly either!'

The kindergarten teacher asked the children if any of their parents or brothers and sisters played a musical instrument. Excitedly one young boy got to his feet and said very seriously, 'My Dad can play a record player.'

How did you cope with the new teacher today?
*She had to cope with us.*

My sewing teacher is a sew and sew.

Did you hear about the unpopular teacher who made a spectacle of himself?

*His pupils were highly dilated.*

My teacher used to be a werewolf but she's howl right now.

One day a boy went to school. When he saw his teacher he said:

'Teacher, I found a penguin in the park on Saturday. What shall I do with it?'

'Take it to the zoo tonight.'

The next day, the boy came back.

'Teacher, I took it to the zoo last night. Tonight I'm taking it to the pictures.'

Did you hear about the boy who rang his teacher to say he'd lost his voice?

What has a teacher got that we haven't?
  *The answer book.*

What is the best thing to give the teacher as a parting gift?
  *A comb.*

What do you call teachers with chalk dust in their ears?
  *Anything you like 'cos they can't hear you.*

Relief teachers are so called because it is such a relief when they leave.

I was teacher's pet;
she couldn't afford a dog.

The teacher took his seat at a staff meeting, but was told to put it back.

What did the hungry teacher do?
> *Kept walking till he was fed up.*

Why did the bald teacher paint rabbits on his head?
> *He thought they would look like hares (hairs) from a distance.*

TEACHER: How many feet are there in a yard?
ANDY: It depends on how many people there are in the yard.

TEACHER: What would you have if you had 10p in one pocket and 50p in the other pocket?
JOHNNY: Somebody else's trousers.

Why are teachers rather special?
> *Because they are usually in a class of their own.*

### *Fiendish French* by Miles Kington

*Virtuoso bassist with Instant Sunshine and World Expert on the Ancient and Unacknowledged Art of Speaking Franglais, Miles Kington had the basic principles of the French language drummed into him at Bilton Grange, Rugby, and Glenalmond School, Perthshire.*

I find it very difficult telling jokes to French people. Not because French is very difficult (it isn't very difficult: it's impossible), but because the French have no sense of humour. Here is a simple conversation.

ME: What is black and white, and flies through space at amazing speeds?

FRENCHMAN: Je ne sais pas exactement.

ME: Supernun!

FRENCHMAN: Je ne comprends pas.

Of course, this may be because the Frenchman does not understand English. So let us try again.

MOI: Qu'est-ce qui est blanc et noir, et vole dans l'espace à des vitesses tout à fait mind-boggling et fantastiques?

FRANÇAIS: C'est facile. Le Space Shuttle. Ou une zèbre en orbite. Ou une liquorice toute-sorte intergalactique.

MOI: Non. Supernonne!

FRANCAIS: Je ne comprends pas.

The best thing to do is to teach a Frenchman to speak English and then tell him a joke, but this may take several years, by which time you've probably forgotten the joke.

So the only thing you can really do is remember that the French think that the English have a fantastic sense of humour. English humour is famous throughout the world, especially in places where they do not speak English. So when you want to amuse a Frenchman, say something – anything – and then roar with laughter. He will be afraid to admit he does not understand and he too will roar with laughter.

A lot of English humour depends on adding little phrases to what the other person has just said, like, 'That's the story of my life' or 'As the bishop said to the actress'. It might be a good idea to have a store of these phrases in French.

C'est l'histoire de ma vie.

Nudge, nudge, wink, wink, ne dis plus.

Comme l'évêque dit à l'actrice.

You could always try doing knock, knock jokes in French ...

VOUS. Knock, knock.

FRANÇAIS: Qui est là?

VOUS: Harry.

FRANÇAIS: Harry qui?

VOUS: Haricot vert!! (*roar with laughter*)

FRANÇAIS: Je ne comprends pas.

And, as a last resort, there are always Irish jokes. The French don't have Irish jokes, only Belgian jokes, which are the same as Irish jokes except they are told about the Belgians.

YOU: What's black and white and can't get off the ground?

FRENCHMAN: Je ne sais pas.

YOU: Belgian Supernun!

FRENCHMAN: Ha ha! Hou ha ha! Très drôle!

What's funny about that, you may ask. Nothing very much. I told you the French have no sense of humour. Good luck!

TEACHER: Janet, what did the Normans say when they saw the cliffs of Dover?
JANET: Cor, Anglais.

TEACHER: I wish you'd pay a little attention to your French.
PUPIL: I'm paying as little as possible.

There was a class having a lesson and one boy said, 'Miss, can we do French now?'
The teacher replied, 'Mais oui.'
The boy said, 'Sorry, *may we* do French now?'

PUPIL: What is the capital of France?
TEACHER: Don't know.
PUPIL: F, I would say.

TEACHER: Où est le pain, Tommy?
TOMMY: Le pain is in my knee, Miss.

TEACHER: Translate for me 'L'Anglais avec son sang-froid habituel.'
PUPIL: Easy. 'The Englishman with his usual bloody cold.'

TEACHER: How do you know Joan of Arc was French?
PUPIL: She was Maid in France!

Frappe, frappe.
Qui est là?
Lors.
Lors qui?
That's why I'm knocking at the door.

Napoleon and Wellington were having a pre-battle drink when Wellington suddenly realized that it was nearly time to start fighting. Raising his glass, he proposed a toast: 'To the water. It is the hour.'

Napoleon repeated the toast in French ... 'A l'eau. C'est l'heure.'

TEACHER: What does *coup de grâce* mean?
PUPIL: It's French for lawn mower, Sir.

A teacher giving a French lesson saw a pupil asleep. He said 'The person who was asleep, report to me after class.' And fourteen people turned up.

Our French teacher is so thick that he thinks *C'est un stylo* is a French barber.

BOY: Our new French teacher has got a funny voice.
MUM: Oh dear.
BOY: One minute she talks English, the next she talks Double Dutch.

BOY: Miss, why are we having frogs for dinner?
DINNER LADY: Your teacher told me you were doing a project on France, so I thought I'd help you.

There were three cats named Un, Deux and Trois.
One day they went rowing, and what happened?
Un, Deux, Trois cats sank.

Conversation overheard by a teacher:
CHRIS: I'm glad I wasn't born in France.
COLIN: Why?
CHRIS: I can't speak French.

Latin's a dead language,
As dead as dead can be.
It killed off all the Romans
And now it's killing me.

A French student was coming to stay with us. We met her in Dublin and decided to bring her into Switzer's for coffee. But she was very reluctant to go into the shop, and kept pointing at the word SALE on the window. My big sister figured it all out. SALE in French means dirty.

A schoolboy jumped into the river in Paris in an attempt to kill himself. He was said to be 'in Seine'.

*Translations:*

| | |
|---|---|
| *Mal de mer* | Mail the horse |
| *Coup de grâce* | Cut the grass |
| *Poussinière* | The cat's in there |
| *Défense d'afficher* | Defend the fish |
| *Ouvrez la fenêtre* | Hoover the furniture |
| *Entrez* | On the tray |
| *Moi aussi* | I am Australian |

What do French people eat for breakfast?
> *Huit heures bix.*

What's the difference between a French student and an English student?
> *Hundreds of miles.*

What do you get when you cross 1 and 2 in French?
*Under.*

My French teacher is called Miss Gun but, by the way she talks, she should be called Miss Bullet.

What jumps up and down, then croaks like a frog but isn't a frog?
*A French teacher.*

A boy was having his very first French lesson. He didn't understand a word that the teacher was saying. He then put up his hand and asked, 'Miss, can I please go to the toilet?'

'Oui oui,' answered the teacher.

'No, Miss, just a drink of water.'

There was a French teacher in France, and she asked her pupils 'How do you think the Eiffel Tower got its name?'

One boy put his hand up and said, 'I know – there was a drunk man and he began to climb the Tower. When he had nearly reached the top, his hands began to slip and he said, "I know now why they call it I fall tower."'

Why do French people eat frogs?
*Because they've got hopping good taste.*

What's French, very wobbly, tall and tasty?
*The Trifle Tower.*

There was a girl sitting in the dining hall eating some chips, and she said to the dinner lady, 'Miss, I don't like the look of those chips, they're all blue, white and red!'

The dinner lady replied, 'Well what do you expect? They're French fries!'

What is the French National Anthem?
*Mayonnaise.*

TEACHER: What do French people do to make people cry?
BEN: Sell them onions.

What do French children say when they have just had school dinners?
*'Mercy!'*

# *Horrible*
# *Homework*

## Horrible Homework by
## Janet Street-Porter

*Journalist and television presenter Janet Street-Porter's
schools were Peterborough Primary School, Fulham, and
Lady Margaret Comprehensive, Fulham.*

One of my earliest memories of homework is being kept
behind after school because I was the last person in the
class to learn to write with one of those ghastly dip
pens. Although I could write perfectly with a pencil I
was told that I would bring disgrace on my primary
school in my 11-plus exam unless I could master pen
and ink. I was made to take horrid writing cards home
with me and spend hours on the kitchen table doing
lines of loops followed by lines of Ws. One result was
that I nearly got blood poisoning from the ink that
permanently covered all the fingers of my left hand;
another long-term effect was to make my writing like
that on the cards – the horrid, arty, 'designed' variety.
Even now I wish I could write like other people, but it
still comes out looking like writing cards.

I went to primary and then grammar school in
Fulham, in West London. When I was fifteen my family
moved to Perivale in Middlesex, but I still travelled to
school in Fulham on the Underground every day. A lot
of homework got done on the tube, and if I got really
bogged down I'd often look up and find I'd ended up in
West Ruislip, having struggled through some awful
Latin translation. I think I must have been the worst
Latin student ever. I'd spend hours on the tube silently
learning the set books, only to get my homework sent

back time after time. The English and General Studies essays I did on the tube didn't fare any better either.

When I started to write this piece I went down into my cellar and found my homework books, smelling of damp and covered with ink blots and red messages from teachers like 'Please see me – this *just will not do*.' You can see London Transport's contribution: all the writing slopes in the direction of the train. I also found a notebook in which I recorded how much homework I actually did. I just can't understand it … two and a half hours of maths on a Tuesday, followed by a history essay on Wednesday that also took two and a half hours. I find this hard to believe as I have also recently discovered my diaries for the same year and they are full

of such riveting information as 'Saw Terry down the chip shop' and 'Put £2 down on leather jacket', not to mention 'Went out dancing and met John'. How did I fit all this exciting stuff in?

Reading through my English essays I found one or two subjects that positively inspired me; one was entitled 'Escape from school' and another called 'My views on television'. One essay was about what I would take on a desert island: I chose a hammer, a piano, some nails and a book about plants, as well as the Bible. The teacher was totally unimpressed by this bit of sucking-up and wrote 'Do not ever use a ballpoint pen.' I suppose I should have told her I'd be taking a pen, ink and writing cards on the stupid desert island.

TEACHER: Joe, your homework seems to be in your father's handwriting.
JOE: Yes, Miss, I used his pen.

TEACHER: Your homework sum was if a man swims four miles in one hour, how long would it take him to swim 25 miles? Why haven't you done it, Tommy?
TOMMY: My father isn't back yet, Sir!

DAD: Son, would you like any help with your homework tonight?
SON: No thanks, Dad, you only got one out of ten last night.

A boy got stuck on his history homework, so he asked his dad, 'Dad, can you tell me a bit about the Iron Age?'
'Sorry, son, I'm a bit rusty on that!'

BOY: Dad, I can't do my English. What's *unaware*?
DAD: It's the last thing you take off at night.

TEACHER: Tom, your homework is getting better.
TOM: I know, my dad's stopped helping me.

TEACHER: Simon, where's your homework?
SIMON: I haven't got it.
TEACHER: Why not?
SIMON: My dad can't do those sums.

BOY: Dad, we've got to name six things with milk in them, for homework.
DAD: Chocolate, rice, icecream, three cows!

TEACHER: Is your homework in?
PUPIL: No, it's in the dustbin.
TEACHER: Why?
PUPIL: You said it was a piece of rubbish.

BOY: Dad, how do space platforms stay in space?
FATHER: Well, I don't know much about space, son.
*Five minutes later:*
BOY: Dad, how do bombs explode?
FATHER: Well – I don't know much about bombs.
BOY: Dad – am I disturbing you?
FATHER: Not at all. You have to ask questions if you want to learn anything!

TEACHER: John, I'm able to read one of the essays you did for homework, but the other is very poor.
JOHN: Yes, Sir, my mother is a much better writer than my father.

A small boy was doing his homework, and said to his father, 'Dad, where is the Pennine Chain?'
'I don't know, Son, ask your mother, she puts everything away.'

What did one maths book say to the other?
    *I've got problems.*

What happened to the boy who did his homework with sticky hands?
    *He got stuck in the middle of a sum.*

SON: Dad, will you help me find the lowest common denominator in this homework problem?

DAD: Good heavens, Son, don't tell me that hasn't been found yet – they were looking for it when I was a kid!

TEACHER: Sammy, your homework tonight is to write an essay on a horse.

SAMMY: OK, Sir.

*That evening:*

FARMER: What are you doing sitting on that horse with a pencil and paper in your hand?

SAMMY: My teacher told me to write an essay on a horse.

FATHER: Son, do you want any help with your homework?

SON: No thanks, Dad, I'll get it wrong on my own.

TEACHER: What happened to your homework?

PUPIL: I made it into a paper plane and somebody hijacked it!

TEACHER: I told you to do a two-page essay on cricket but you've only done three lines. Why?

BOY: Rain stopped play, Sir.

TEACHER: I asked for a two-page composition about milk. Your paper is only half a page long.

PUPIL: That's right – I wrote about condensed milk.

TEACHER: Did you write this poem all by yourself?

PUPIL: Every line of it, Miss.

TEACHER: Well, pleased to meet you, William Shakespeare.

TEACHER: You seem to have been confused in your history and maths homework.

BOY: Why, Sir?

TEACHER: I asked you what you knew about Gregory the Great, and you wrote that he was in a square in Rome, and said 'We've got some right angles here.'

TEACHER: Fred, come here.

FRED: Yes, Miss?

TEACHER: For your homework I asked for a sentence using the word *climate*.

FRED: I did – the mountain was so steep I couldn't climate.

TEACHER: I want the whole class to bring me their home-work first thing in the morning.
PUPIL: Sir, how can I carry the hoover and the dishes to school?

TEACHER: Why didn't you look for your homework book, Jimmy?
JIMMY: I was afraid.
TEACHER: Afraid of what?
JIMMY: Afraid I might find it, Sir!

What is so bad we get it every night?
　　　*Homework*.

TEACHER: Where's your homework?
CHILD: At home.
TEACHER: Why?
CHILD: Schoolwork is left at school, so homework is left at home.

PUPIL: Please Miss, my homework was to draw a gun.
TEACHER: So?
PUPIL: I shot my sister.

The teacher said to the pupil, 'Write a project on Elizabeth I or Alfred the Great.'
　　'Sir, I'd rather write on paper!'

SIMON: People are right about *Grange Hill* teaching children violence.
GARY: Why?
SIMON: Because I was watching *Grange Hill* and I didn't do my homework, and the teacher hit me for not doing it.

'Your homework for today is to write a sentence about the war.'

'Why just a sentence, Miss?'

'Because that's all you'll write anyway.'

HEAD TEACHER: What did you say to your teacher that made her faint, lad?

BOY: I told her I'd done my homework.

PETER: Tom, what is your favourite subject for homework?

TOM: Oh, English. What's yours?

PETER: I like doing nothing.

TOM: We never get that!

PETER: I know, but there's no reason why I can't like it!

SON: I'm fed up with homework. I want to be a pop star and get on the TV.

FATHER: Well, hop up on top then!

MOTHER: John's teacher says he ought to have an encyclopedia.

FATHER: Let him walk to school same as I did.

BOY: Dad, I don't want to do my homework.

FATHER: Why? No one has died of it yet.

BOY: Well, why should I be the first to risk it?

I'm doing a project on trains – I have to keep track of everything!

Jimmy was a very religious boy. He would never do homework if there was a Sunday in the week.

What book fights you while you are trying to do your homework?

    *A scrap-book.*

*Homework* by Anne Sirs

For homework, a religious studies teacher said, 'Write a sentence using the word *incarnation*.'

    This is what a boy wrote: 'Sometimes I use milk in my coffee, but sometimes I put in Carnation!'

For homework I had a crossword puzzle. Boy, did it make me angry!

Asked to write an essay on water, Little Willie thought for a moment and then wrote, 'Water is a colourless liquid that turns dark when you wash it.'

TOM: What have you done for your science homework?
NICK: Ring around a neutron,
       A pocket full of protons.
       A fission, a fusion,
       We all fall down!

What's the most magic homework?
    *Spellings.*

Why is a boy who studies hard like a fly killer?
    *Because he's a swotter.*

Why is homework always boring?
    *Because it makes holes in your free time.*

# Ugly
# Uniform

## Ugly Uniform by Ruth Davies

*Playing Penny Lewis in the BBC series* Grange Hill, *Ruth Davies had plenty of memories to help her from her days at Primrose Hill Primary School, London and the Italia Conti Stage School.*

At the age of eleven I found myself in a happy frame of mind at the prospect of wearing the Italia Conti Stage School uniform. I was a little shocked, though, by its lack of imagination. Since it's a stage school, I rather expected to wear a really theatrical outfit: like sombreros, sequined dresses and Dracula capes for the girls, and army surplus gear for the boys. Instead we were issued with dowdy clothes which made everyone look horribly alike – mainly horrible. However, once past the stage of feeling stupid, it became quite fun, adding one's own personal touches to the hideous outfit! I remember the regulation navy blue jumpers gradually transformed into turquoise cardigans, and low black patent shoes into stilettos. The emblems on our blazers were hidden by badges and the girls' hats were reshaped into more flattering styles. But our uniform proved to have its limitations when we tried to adjust to the latest punk fashion!

We were lectured by teachers on how to conduct ourselves while in uniform, because we were representing our school. We were forbidden to eat sweets or draw attention to ourselves on public transport, or shed layers as soon as we got outside the school gates. Of course we did all of these things and gained a St Trinian-like reputation. Far from fading into the background, the uniform stuck out like a three-legged man and we had to be escorted to the tube train because the local kids were always rushing out to attack us.

I was unfortunate enough to have to wear two uniforms at this time, my own when I was at school, and that of Grange Hill when I was filming the series. It was even worse having to wear a pretend one, but at least it was comforting to depict a girl who fought for the abolition of it. Penny Lewis wasn't an exceptional or daring dresser and school uniform helped disguise this, but, for those of us who think clothes are an extension of character, a uniform is a bit of a drag. My advice to frustrated uniform-wearers is not to take it all too seriously – it's a joke in itself!

PUPIL: Please, Miss, do we have to wear uniform?

TEACHER: Yes, so you'll all look alike.

PUPIL: Good, then if I do something bad it must have been somebody else, and if somebody else does something good, it must be me.

What do you get if you cross a vicar with our school uniform?

*Holy clothes.*

I wouldn't say our school is like a prison, but we've got little arrows on our uniform.

1 ST BOY: Why do schools have black uniform?
2 ND BOY: I don't know. Why?
1 ST BOY: Because school is dead boring.

JOHNNY: Miss, why aren't we allowed to wear black and white striped trousers?
TEACHER: Because the cars will mistake you for a zebra crossing.

A boy came home from school and said to his mother, 'The new headmaster said that after seeing us at dinner we would be having a new school uniform next year.'

'What colour?' asked his mother.

'It will be a custard-coloured tie with rice-coloured spots, a gravy-coloured blazer and chocolate-sauce-coloured trousers.'

Why do children at high school wear ties?
*So they can strangle their teachers.*

BOY: What is blue and white, looks like a snake, and hangs around your neck?
GIRL: A school tie.

What is red, grey, red, grey?
*A school tie rolling down the hill.*

What is grey and hairy?
*A school jumper.*

TEACHER: Where's your uniform?
JIMMY: At home, Miss.
TEACHER: Then go home and get it on.
*Later:*
TEACHER: Jimmy, you're wet!
JIMMY: Well, my uniform was in the wash at the time.

BOY: I'm not going to wear a school uniform.
FRIEND: Why not?
BOY: 'Cos I haven't got one!

TEACHER: Where's your school cap?
PUPIL: In my pocket, Miss.
TEACHER: It's all tattered.
PUPIL: It got hit by a ball.
TEACHER: What sort of ball?
PUPIL: A moth ball.

TEACHER: Philip, where is your cap?
PHILIP: The cook thought it was beef and we had it for school dinner.

TEACHER: James, where did you get that Easter tie from?
JAMES: What makes you think it's an Easter tie?
TEACHER: Well, it's got egg on it.

TEACHER: Jim, you'd better pull your socks up
JIM: But, Miss, they were ankle socks the other day, and you keep on asking me to pull them up and now they're leg warmers.

A boy came into school with very dirty shoes.
   'Did you clean your shoes this morning?' asked the teacher.
   'No.'
   'No what?' snapped his teacher.
   'No blooming boot polish.'

What do you call a jacket on fire?
        *A blazer!*

What did the blazer say to the mackintosh?
        '*Belt up!*'

Knock, knock.
Who's there?
Una.
Una who?
Uniform inspector.

TEACHER: Your uniform is filthy! What would you say if I came to school with egg on my tie and ink stains all over my blazer?
BOY: I'd be too polite to mention it, Sir.

*Boy's Uniform* by B. Lazer

TEACHER: Susan, why aren't you wearing uniform?

SUSAN: Because I don't feel like it!

TEACHER: I will deal with you later, along with the headmistress.

SUSAN: Why, didn't she wear uniform either?

JANE: My teacher told me that I've been so good this week that I don't have to wear my school hat any more.

DAD: What hat? You haven't got a hat, have you?

JANE: Yes Dad, the Dunce's hat!

'Miss, do we have to wear school uniform for this year's school outing?'
   'Why?'
   'Well, I'd rather look smart for a change.'

Why do Hornsey girls wear red?
   *To warn the teachers they're dangerous.*

What do female sheep wear?
   *Ewe-niforms.*

What did the tie say to the hat?
   '*You go on a head, while I hang around.*'

What did one uniform say to the other?
   '*Shall we let them in today?*'

# Canny
# Caretakers

## Canny Caretakers by Rod Hull

*No stranger to jokes like these, Rod Hull went to
Rose Street Primary School and Sheerness Technical
School.*

I like school caretakers – they're a race apart. My earliest
recollections of school are of the caretaker at Rose
Street Primary School, Sheerness, in Kent. Taken there
by my mother a day before school term began in order to
meet the headmistress, I can remember clutching Mum's
hand tightly as we walked through the school gates. I
must admit, it didn't look too bad. The playground was
empty (quite unlike what it would be the following day)
and so we walked around in the sunshine waiting for the
time of the appointment while I suspiciously eyed the
large, yellow brick building which I knew would house
me for the next (seemingly) umpteen years.

It was then that we met the Caretaker. He popped up
from some stone stairs leading down to what looked like
a cave. Actually, it was a boiler-room, but to me it was a
cave.

'Hello,' he said, wiping his hands with a piece of rag
and then tucking it into the pocket of his oily blue
overalls. 'Coming to school, are you?' I nodded. I was
very shy.

Then he bent down to my height. 'Would you like to
see a hedgehog?' he said mysteriously. I'd never seen a
hedgehog. I'm not quite sure I would have known what
a hedgehog was at four years old, but I accepted his
invitation and gladly followed him down the stone steps
and into the Cave – still clutching Mum's hand, of
course.

It was lovely in that Cave and the hedgehog was beautiful. It was kept in a little cardboard box tucked behind the back of the boiler. I was actually allowed to *touch* the boiler, tap the dials and inspect the whole Cave with the Caretaker showing me around like I was the only friend he had. I noticed the cleaning rags and

brooms and buckets, the pile of gardening tools in the corner, the chair with a cushion on it next to a table on which stood a teapot, a bottle of milk, a teacup and saucer and a little gas-ring supporting a huge kettle that was steaming away merrily. How lovely it all was! If coming to school meant I could learn things and grow up and become a caretaker, then I was certainly looking forward to it.

I realize now, many years later, what a great service that man did for me, and probably lots more like me. It certainly took away the fear of going to school for the first time, of leaving home (I only lived just down the street!), of not getting back until tea-time (probably 3.30) and suddenly being thrown in with a whole lot of kids I'd never met before. None of this bothered me. I was off to see my Friend and I even took some bread for the hedgehog.

And so my school days began and with them, I suppose, the shaping of my life and career. I finally qualified as an engineer, travelled to Australia, gave up engineering, became a scriptwriter, worked in a television studio, became a stage performer, travelled the world again and now I've ended up back here – eight miles from Rose Street Primary School, where I learnt my first valuable lesson: friendship.

Many's the time I cast my mind back to that friendly Cave: the whitewashed walls to keep you cool in the summer, the boiler going and the kettle bubbling on the gas-ring to keep you snug in winter. My Friend didn't have to go off searching for fame and fortune; he had it all there. The Cave was his fortune and his fame ... well, his fame was being the Caretaker.

What did the caretaker say when the mud spat?
    *'You dirty thing.'*

What goes droom droom?
    *A caretaker gone wrong.*

What is the difference between a biscuit and a caretaker?
    *You can't dip a caretaker in your tea.*

We have a caretaker called Will Knott. He is so lazy he
    never does anything for anybody. What do you think
    we call him?
    *Won't!*

Why is a caretaker's job never done?
    *Because he never starts it.*

*Classroom Cracks* by Polly Filla
*Measuring Classrooms* by S. Timate
*Caretaker's Work* by Clare Inup
*Hole in My Bucket* by Lee King
*Scrubbing Floors* by Neil Ling Down

Our caretaker often gets the pip: His name is Mr Lemon.

Our school has the lowest rate of vandalism in the borough. The caretaker locks the teachers in the staffroom.

'Look here,' said the headmaster, 'if you can't do your work better I'll have to get another man.'

'Thank you, Sir,' said the caretaker, 'I could do with an assistant.'

What do you get if you cross a caretaker with an elephant?
*A ten-ton corridor sweeper.*

HEADMASTER: That new caretaker is lazy.
SECRETARY: Yes, Sir, slow in everything.
HEADMASTER: No, not in everything. He gets tired quickly.

'I've just crossed a caretaker with a monk who smokes.'
'What did you get?'
'A caretaker with a bad habit.'

Why couldn't the caretaker lock the doors?
>    *Because the children had bolted.*

CARETAKER: Hey, stop writing on the wall.
BOYS: Don't worry, it's invisible ink.

As two boys were passing their school a caretaker leaned over the wall and showed them a ball.
    'Is this yours?' he asked.
    'Did it do any damage?' said one of the boys.
    'No,' replied the caretaker.
    'Then it's mine.'

What's red and puffs out smoke?
>    *An angry caretaker.*

I say, I say, I say, who goes to school each day, but doesn't learn anything?
>    *Our caretakers.*

There was a young caretaker named Frank,
Who kept all his beer in the school tank.
One day it was locked,
And he was so shocked,
Because without his pint he'd go blank.

What did the caretaker say when he lost his broom?
>    *'Oh drat, I won't be able to sweep the dirt under the mat now.'*

What did the mop say to the caretaker?
>    *'Don't squeeze me so tight!'*

Why did the caretaker give up his job?
>    *Because he found that grime doesn't pay!*

CARETAKER: Why are you crying?

SUSIE: I've lost five pence.

CARETAKER: Here is five pence for you. Now why are you crying?

SUSIE: If I hadn't lost five pence I'd have ten pence now!

Our Headmaster thinks that Mr Sheen is the caretaker.

HEAD TEACHER: I notice you don't cut your grass any longer.

CARETAKER: No, I cut it shorter.

TEACHER: Murphy Minor – why have you got your fingers painted green?

MURPHY MINOR: Because the caretaker told me if I wanted to help him in the garden I would have to have green fingers.

One boy said to his friend, 'I think the caretaker must be a good footballer.'

'Why?'

'Well I heard one of the dinner ladies say that he was a good sweeper and he was always ready to strike. I think that he's going to be transferred.'

'How do you know?'

'She said that he'd probably be sent to Coventry.'

Knock, knock.

Who's there?

Arthur.

Arthur who?

Arthur any more jobs around the school?

Our caretaker is called Angus McOatup.

'Our caretaker is 95 years old and he's still not got a grey hair.'
'Why?'
'Because he's bald.'

CARETAKER: I'll teach you to throw stones at my greenhouse.
BOY: I wish you would. I had ten shots and haven't hit it yet.

Have you heard the one about the stupid caretaker who was asked to prepare the football pitch for the match, so he scrubbed off all the white lines?

ANGRY HEADMASTER: Why are you late again today?
CARETAKER: I'm afraid I overslept.
ANGRY HEADMASTER: You mean you sleep at home as well?

Why did the pretty schoolteacher marry the caretaker?
*Because he swept her off her feet.*

It was open day at school, and a small boy had lost his mother. The caretaker saw the boy crying, so he asked him, 'What's the matter, son?'

'I've lost my mum,' said the boy.

'What's your mum like?' asked the caretaker.

'Guinness and bingo.'

# Traumatic
## Trips

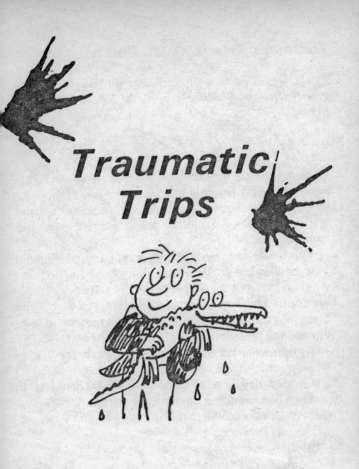

## *Traumatic Trips* by Alan Coren

*Alan Coren is Editor of* Punch. *His schools were Osidge Primary School, Southgate, and East Barnet Grammar School.*

Whenever I hear, these days, the *hee-haw-hee-haw* of police cars as they hurtle fore and aft of one of those enormous green coaches which roar prisoners on their way to court, the years roll back and school trips fill the memory.

*We* should have been in transport like that for school trips: bars on the windows, treble-locks on the doors, warning sirens to the innocent public, and each child handcuffed to some granite-muscled master with a judo black belt holding up his trousers and a truncheon in his hip pocket!

A couple of hard-eyed Alsatians sitting in the luggage racks wouldn't have been a bad idea, either.

Cooped up in school, we were relatively harmless: the teachers knew every inch of the territory and, if outnumbered, could whistle up support and corner us.

But once outside, on unfamiliar, unboundaried ground, like Kew Gardens, the London Zoo, Box Hill or Hatfield House, the teachers didn't stand a chance. The coach doors would hiss open, and forty terrible tiny things would launch themselves, shrieking, into a landscape equally strange to the two teachers who had been stuck with our impossible supervision.

If a master was lucky enough to grab the two boys who were chucking gravel at the tigers, he missed the two who were smoking in the dark aquarium; if he caught the one who was putting his own inky signature to a priceless painting in Lord Gumboyle's library, he failed to spot the one who was sticking a plasticine moustache on the bust of Lady Gumboyle in the Great Hall; if he managed to get the fire brigade to remove the three who had somehow managed to climb onto the roof of the Cactus House, he wasn't around to notify the police of the four who had chopped down the oldest magnolia in England.

And shall I ever forget that wonderful moment, thirty years ago, when Class 3a visited St Paul's, with an enthusiastic history master springing up the three hundred steps to the Great Dome, confident that forty small boys were traipsing eagerly after, straining for his every word, only to find, when he reached the top, that there was no one behind him at all? They were all a hundred feet below, strung out around the Whispering Gallery, making the poor old cathedral echo and blush with the filthiest whispers they could think of.

They all grew up, of course; and perhaps most of them outgrew their villainy, too. But just occasionally, when those green coaches thunder by and I glance up at the windows, it occurs to me that one or two of the adult faces peering out from behind the bars are not, perhaps, entirely unfamiliar.

BOY: Will I be going on the school trip, Sir?
TEACHER: Yes, if you don't behave yourself.

TEACHER: There's a school trip coming up.
GIRL: Where to?
TEACHER: France.
GIRL: How much?
TEACHER: £31.
GIRL: I can't afford that.
TEACHER: It's not for you – it's for us teachers to get away from you lot.

There were two boys on a school trip to the zoo, and they were standing near a lion's cage.
SIMON: Once I saw a man-eating lion in a zoo.
TIM: So what? I saw a man eating fish in a cafe.

The class were on a nature trail, when Jimmy said to the teacher, 'What has eight legs, six eyes, pink spots and purple spikes down its back?'

The teacher replied, 'I've never heard of such a thing.'

'Well,' said Jimmy, 'there's one on your collar right now.'

BILL: Did you go on the school trip?
SID: Yeah.
BILL: What was the best bit?
SID: Going home!

On a trip to the art gallery the teacher saw a boy slapping a statue.

TEACHER: Why are you slapping that statue, boy?

BOY: Just before you came in, Sir, a gallery attendant came up to me and said, 'Beat it kid'.

A class went to Rome. On one Sunday they went to a Roman church. On returning, a teacher asked them if they had behaved.

One girl replied, 'Oh yes, Sir. A kind gentleman offered me a plate full of money, but I said, "No, thanks."'

A teacher told his class that he wanted some responsible children to go to the Commonwealth Institute.

A girl replied, 'You can put me down, Sir, because on every trip I go on something gets damaged and I'm always responsible.'

A party of schoolchildren went for a trip in the country and one of them found a pile of empty milk bottles.

'Look Miss, I've found a cow's nest.'

We went on a school trip to London. One boy got lost. Our teacher asked a policeman had he seen a boy with a wooden leg called Mark?

'What's the other leg called?' asked the puzzled bobby.

TEACHER (*on a trip to the museum*): Look at this huge grizzly bear, class. Can anyone tell me if we get fur from the grizzly?

JIMMY: I'd get as fur from him as possible!

Billy came home from a school camping trip.

'Did your tent leak?' asked his father.

'Only when it rained,' said Billy.

A girl said to her father, 'At assembly today our headmaster said "we shall fight on the beaches, we shall fight on the airfields, we shall fight in the streets".'

'Ah yes,' said her father, 'those are the immortal words of Sir Winston Churchill.'

'Oh, I thought he was telling us about our school trip to France.'

FRED: On our last school trip, the school bus got a puncture.

JOE: How did it happen?

FRED: There was a fork in the road.

MOTHER: Did you enjoy your school trip?

PAULA: Oh yes. We're going again tomorrow.

MOTHER: Why?

PAULA: Search party.

MARK: Where did all the cuts and blood come from?
PETER: The school went on a trip.

MOTHER: Did you have a nice trip today?
SON: Yes, that's why I'm limping.

BOY: Are we going on a trip this year?
TEACHER: Yes.
BOY: Where are we going?
TEACHER: To see the apes.
BOY: Where's that.
TEACHER: Right here.
BOY: I'm pretending to be one of those apes.
TEACHER: You don't need to.

A teacher went to the railway booking office and asked for one adult and 22 child return tickets.
'Where to?' asked the booking clerk.
'Back here, you idiot!' replied the teacher.

On our school trips we often go for a tramp in the woods. Fortunately for the tramp we don't often find him.

Where's the worst trip you are likely to take?
*To the headmaster's office.*

A class went on a school trip to the Sahara Desert. After two weeks, why didn't they go hungry?
*Because of the sand-which-is there.*

On a school trip to France, at dinner.
BOY: Have you got frog's legs?
WAITER: Yes, certainly.
BOY: Well, hop into the kitchen and get me fish and chips.

Why did one school trip take longer than the other and they were going to same place at the same time?

*One coach was going faster than the other.*

*Chinese School Trips* by Hwan Missing
*Trips* by C. U. Agayne
*A Day Out to the White House* by M. Bassador
*A Trip to the Haunted House* by Hugo First

Do you know what happened when the pregnant teacher took her class on a school trip?

*She had trip-lets.*

TEACHER: Now class, we are going on a trip to the zoo. If you get frightened when you see an adder, just subtract it.

There was a teacher from China,
Who took a trip on an ocean liner.
She slipped on the deck
And twisted her neck,
Now she can see what's going on behind her.

The school cruise was a great success but a lot of people had to be turned away. The raft only held 15 people.

TEACHER: And why did you and your brother hand in exactly the same essay on your trip to the zoo?
PUPIL: Same trip, Miss.

Two classes were going on an excursion down to the stream.
1ST BOY: How many fish did you catch?
2ND BOY: I can't count.
1ST BOY: I don't have any fish to count.

After a school visit to the circus, George and the teacher were talking about the acts.

'I didn't think much of the knife thrower, did you?' said George.

'I thought he was super,' said the teacher.

'Well, I didn't,' said George, 'He kept chucking those knives at that soppy girl, and never hit her once . . .'

What will we see in the middle of Paris when we go on the school trip?
> *The letter R.*

What is a Lap Lander?
> *A clumsy girl on a school bus.*

KATE: Mummy, Mummy, I need a ladder for school.
MOTHER: What for?
KATE: Teacher says we're going on a climbing holiday.

# List of Contributing Schools

# List of Contributing Schools

We have done our best to include all the schools that sent jokes for this collection and apologize for any that may have been left out.

Aberdare Welsh School
Abingdon Primary School
Alexandra Junior School
Allerton Junior School,
　class LJ3
Amberfield School, *lower 3*
Ann Edwards School
Aspley Player Junior East
　School

Baden-Powell Middle School,
　*class 4*
Ballyclare Primary School,
　*class P4B*
Ballykelly Primary School,
　*class 5R*
Beaufort County Middle
　School, *class 4*
Bellevue Junior School
Bentinck School
Benton Park Primary School,
　*reception class, infant 1 and 2*
Bishop Eaton J. M. I. School,
　*class 3*
Blaen y Maes Junior School
Bolton on Swale C. of E.
　Primary School, *class J3*

Brownedge St Mary's R.C.
　High School, *1st year*
Burton Bradstock School, *class 1*
Bushey Middle School, *class 3K*

Carlton-le-Willows
　Comprehensive School
Catton Grove Middle School,
　*class 3*
Christ the King School
Christchurch Church-in-Wales
　School, *Miss Reed's class*
Codnor Junior School, *classes
　4 and 7*
Cold Ash St Mark's C. of E.
　School, *class 3*
County High School for Girls,
　Colchester, *form 1F*
Courthouse School, *class 3S*
Crawhall County First School,
　*class 5*
Crieff Primary School,
　*class P7M*
Cubbington C. of E. Combined
　School
Culcheth Hall School for
　Girls, *class J1*

Cults Academy, *class 1.2*

Davenhill Junior School,
 *classes 1, 3, 4, 6, 7, 8, 9 and
 11*
Delabole County Primary
 School
De la Salle College, *class J3*
Devonshire Junior School,
 *class 4*
Dingleside Middle School
Dursley C. of E. Junior School

Eckington C. of E. First
 School, *class 2*
Egerton C. of E. Primary
 School

Garforth Parochial School,
 *class F*
Gastchurch County Primary
 School, *class 1*
Gilling West C. of E. Primary
 School
Glenfield County Junior
 School, *class 7*
Good Shepherd School
Grange First School,
 *amber class*
Great Witchingham School,
 *class 3*
Guildford County School,
 *class 2S*

Hadleigh County Primary
 School, *class J4M*
Hamble County Primary
 School, *class 11*
Harrogate Granby High
 School, *class 1K*
Harrold School

Hartly Brook First School
Hayes Meadow Primary
 School, *class 9*
Helpringham School, *Miss
 Hill's class*
Hermitage Comprehensive
 School, *form 1A2*
Highfield Junior School, *class 4*
Hilton Primary School, *classes
 5, 7, 9, 11 and 13*
Hoghton County Primary
 School, *class J2*
Holly Lodge Comprehensive
 School, *classes 1J, 1L,
 1M/1A3, 1Q, 1S and 2S*
Holly Lodge School,
 Smethwick, *class 4E*
Holy Family Middle School,
 Langley, *class 1/2*
Holy Family School, Warton,
 *class 3*
Holy Trinity Primary School,
 *class 6*
Hopwood House
Hornsey School for Girls, *form
 1L*
Hoveringham Junior School
Hugo Meynell School, *Mrs
 Viggar's class*
Hunstanton County Middle
 School, *class 8*

Ipswich Preparatory School,
 *class A1*

John Ray Junior School, *class 12*
Jubilee First School, *class 4*

King David Primary School
King Edward's Grammar
 School for Girls

Knowsley Brookside School,
*class 5*

Ladysmith Middle School, *class
2E*

Lanchester E. P. Junior School,
*classes 6 and 7*

Larkhall Junior School, *class 1S*

Lawnswood Primary School

Leamington Primary School,
*form JPs*

Leek High School, *forms 1M
and 1N*

Little Bollington C. of E.
Primary School

Ysgol Gyfun Llanhari, *forms 1
and 2*

Loddon County Junior School

Longden C. of E. Primary
School

Lower Kersall Junior School,
*class 4B*

Lowes Wong Junior School,
*class 4B*

Maiden Erleigh School, *class
2E2*

Maidensbridge County Primary
School, *Mrs Easter's class*

Manor Middle School

Manston C. of E. Middle
School

Matthew Holland
Comprehensive School

Maud Heath County Primary
School, *upper juniors*

Melba Primary School,
Australia, *classes 5B, 5S, 6B,
6S and 40P*

Mickle Trafford County
Primary School

Mill View County Primary
School, *class 4P*

Moor Hall Combined School,
*class 7*

Mount Street County Primary
School, *class 4E*

Newlands School, *transition
class*

Nicholas Hawksmoor School

Nineland Lane Junior School

Norbury Manor High School
for Girls, *form 2F*

Norham County First School,
*class II*

Our Lady and St Paul's
Primary School

Our Lady of Lourdes Primary
School, *class P4*

Oxton C. of E. School

Pensby Junior School, *Christine
McGrew's class*

Pershore High School, *class 4H*

Pocklington County Junior
School, *classes 3C and 4T*

Porthcawl Comprehensive
School, *MP English*

Portslade Community College
Lower School

Portsmouth Grammar School,
*form 1M*

Pyrcroft County Middle
School, *class 1/7*

Queen Elizabeth II Primary
School, *primary 7*

Radcliffe-in-Chadderton
School, *class 1L*

Winston Churchill School,
  *2nd year*
Witton Middle School
Wood Green School, *classes 1L,
  1R, 1T, 2L, 2R and 2W*
Woodhouse High School,
  *classes 1R and 3B*
Wombleton C. E. School
Wombridge County Primary
  School, *class 3F*

Woodlands Middle School
Woodnewton School, *juniors*
Worting Junior School
Wribbenhall Middle School

Yarra Valley C. of E. School,
  Australia, *grades 3, 5 and 7*
Yavneh Primary School, *class 3*
Yorkmead School, *class J2*